An Adventure Through End-Time Prophecies

RAY MEDDINGS

WESTBOW
PRESS®
A DIVISION OF THOMAS NELSON
& ZONDERVAN

WestBow Press books may be ordered through booksellers or by contacting:

WestBow Press
A Division of Thomas Nelson & Zondervan
1663 Liberty Drive
Bloomington, IN 47403
www.westbowpress.com
844-714-3454

ISBN: 978-1-6642-8176-9 (sc)
ISBN: 978-1-6642-8177-6 (hc)
ISBN: 978-1-6642-8178-3 (e)

Library of Congress Control Number: 2022919631

Print information available on the last page.

WestBow Press rev. date: 12/20/2022

Chapter 1

Mark 13:23 (Living Bible) Watch out! I have warned you about this ahead of time! Dateline - CoronaVirus pandemic 2020. As I sit here in March 2020, the world is virtually shut down. Death is all around the world and we are in an economic collapse, all within a few weeks. Unemployment is off the charts, and it all started in Wuhan, China, transmitted from a bat to a human or created in a lab, and now it has spread worldwide. In Spain and Italy there are hundreds dying every day.

We know that the Lord God is still on the throne with you, Lord Jesus. You are right beside the Father, who is all knowing. Where are we heading? This is the big question. There are two scripture verses, and one of them is the title of this chapter. Watch out! I have warned you about this ahead of time and I am writing this book to glorify our Father, and to dissect the writings of our God and Savior in Matthew, Mark, Luke, Revelation, Daniel and Ezekiel, and wherever else the Holy Spirit leads me.

The world as a whole is living in a pandemic of sin and corruption. These are the things that Jesus said in Mark 13:23.(Living Bible) Watch out! I have warned you about this ahead of time, and Isaiah 42:9.(Living Bible) Everything I prophesied has come true and now I will prophesy again. I will tell you the future before it happens, Luke 21:28 (NKJ). So, when all these things begin to happen, look up, and lift up your heads,because your redemption (salvation) is nearby.

There are over 300 prophecies in the Old Testament depicting the birth, life and death of Jesus. Let's look at just forty eight of these 300 prophecies and the odds of one man fulfilling these prophecies - prophecies that Jesus fulfilled with 100% accuracy. Let's break down eight of those 300 prophecies. If you cover the state of Texas 2 feet deep with silver dollars, and you mark one of those silver dollars, mix them all up, blindfold a person and have them start walking across the state, the odds of that person finding that marked silver dollar are the same odds that one man could fulfill the prophecies. Fulfilling just eight of those 300 prophecies have the odds of 10 to the 15th power - that's ten with 15 zeros behind it. Now let's take 48 of those prophecies. It is now 10 to the 157th power. What does that mean? It's a 10 with 157 zeros behind it.

Let's break this down according to Emile Borel, with probabilities and life hanging in the balance. One ant traveling at the rate of 1 inch every 15 billion years, if he could carry one atom at a time traveling at that incredibly slow speed, he would be able to move all the atoms in 600,000 trillion= trillion=trillion=trillion universes the size of ours, over 600 trillion light years across the universe. That's why, as in Psalm 14:1(NKJ) The fool has said in his heart, There is no God." There is only one man who fulfilled these prophecies - the God that became man, the second person of the Godhead, the son of God, our savior.

When you construct a building, you have to start with a strong foundation. Let's look at what Jesus said in Matthew 7:24(Living Bible) about building a solid foundation. "Anyone who listens to my teachings and follows it is wise." Like a person who builds a house on solid rock, we must build our lives on Christ. Though the rain comes in torrents, and flood water rise, and the wind beats against that house, it won't collapse because it is built on bedrock. What is Jesus telling us? When the trials and tribulations come upon us, if our lives are built upon Christ and his Word, he will see us through because he is our rock. Psalms 31:2(Living Bible) You are my rock and my fortress. For the honor of your name leads me out of danger. Psalm 28:1 (Living Bible)I pray to you, O Lord my rock. Psalm 104:5(Living Bible) You place the world on its foundation so it would never be moved. Psalm 105:1(Living Bible) Give thanks to the Lord and proclaim his greatness. Then, the last part of Luke 6:49 – But anyone who hears and doesn't obey is like a person who builds a house without a foundation. When the floods sweep down against that house, it will collapse into a heap of ruins. What the Lord is showing us here is another person who built their life in the world, and when the storms of life came this person had built their life on nothing. It's the same as when you built sandcastles on the beach. When the tide reached you, it crumbled everything you had built. The tide rolls in and rolls out again, and everything is gone.

Just as I laid the foundation of chapter 13 of Mark, again, watch out! I have warned you about this ahead of time in my last book. I asked the Lord for one more book and this is it. An Adventure Through End Time Prophecies. As with my other book, I do not know what's ahead or how to get to the final destination. So, let's buckle up like an Indiana Jones adventure. Visualize the best all-terrain vehicle with jacked up, beefy sand tires. It has to be black, stealth-looking and built for adventure. The name on it reads the Holy Bible, so let's rev up that powerhouse engine and load up our supplies like an army reconnaissance mission.

We have our papers from the captain of the Lord's army as we make our way through rough terrain where there will be many twists and turns. We will go through the Book of Revelation, we will make our way through the mountains of Israel to a Valley called Megiddo, to the last battle on earth, where all the worldly forces will be gathered to fight against our great God and Savior. Here, Jesus is going to split the heavens and every eye will see him, as he will come in all his glory. It says that the blood from that battle will be a horse's bridle deep and flow for 200 miles.

No film producer or director could capture this event. Most of us like a great movie. I personally love a good action movie. I like to think it's because I'm a male and it comes with the territory. Growing up in the 50s I enjoyed the black and white cowboy shows like The Rifleman. They were full of action and heroes. When I was reflecting about the current world we live in and how to express my viewpoints, it led me to one of my all-time favorite movies - Indiana Jones. Although Indiana Jones is a series of movies, my favorite was the 1st, Raiders of the lost Ark. When I looked up the movie, I was hit with descriptive words like booby traps, fighting Nazis staring down snakes. On a quest for adventure most of my life as a follower of Christ, it feels similar to being in an action movie. It has been full of twists and turns, epic moments, trials and suffering, but in the midst of my suffering I am reminded of God's grace and His provision over my lifetime. This year has been full of unknowns. We have experienced the pandemic, COVID-19, which is the worst event I have seen in my lifetime.

As we start this adventure with God's hand leading the way, as we dissect His Word, let us focus on Matthew 24:7(NKJ) For nation will rise against nation and Kingdom against Kingdom, and there will be famines, pestilence,(a fatal epidemic disease.) Pestilence is also one the four horsemen of the apocalypse in Revelation. I got this from USA TODAY news, talking about the Asian murder. Hornets originated in China, Southeast Asia and they were found this spring in Washington State. The Department of Agriculture started hunting for them after two confirmed sightings of this predator. They are about 2 inches long, travel 20 miles per hour, and have a stinger about 1/4 of an inch. The sting is 7 times more potent than a regular bee and they are the largest hornet in the world. This invasive hornet slaughters honeybees and can be deadly to humans. This species has raised alarm about spreading further, and now they've just been spotted in the Pacific Northwest. They are an immediate danger to the honeybee population, which is a problem, and they would also attack small birds. The warning is that if they are not eliminated, they are going to be here to stay. It also says that earthquakes will be in various places. All these things are the beginning of sorrows.

Chapter 2

The Search Begins:

Let's slip on our sandals and take a walk with Jesus and the four disciples, as they leave the Temple Mount and travel down through an orchard of olive trees and through a small valley, to a place called the Mount of Olives, then across the valley from the Temple Mount. Peter, James, John and Andrew came to Jesus privately and asked him. "Tell us, when will all this happen? What sign will show us that these things are about to be fulfilled?" Mark 13:3-4(Living Bible) It was Christ's last week on earth before his crucifixion.

The prophetic teachings of Jesus go deeper into the unknown than any of the Old Testament prophets. That's because Jesus knew everything. He spoke to them of things that had been kept secret from the foundation of the world. Jesus knew the Book of Revelation and He sent it to John - one of the four sitting in this group. The timetable for John's writings was around AD 96, and he was answering the questions the disciples were asking Matthew 24:4(NKJ). And Jesus answered and said to them, "Take heed that no one deceives you, (Verse 5) For many will come in My name saying I am the Christ and shall deceive many (Verse 6), And you shall hear of wars and rumors of wars See that you are not troubled. For all these things must come to pass but the end is not yet. There have been deceivers preaching Christ and his coming, and there are false religions in the world we live in today. He had to warn Christians. I read a staggering statistic that 17% of churchgoers spend one hour or less a week in the Word of God, and spend one to two hours in church. I am certainly not pointing any fingers, because there would be 3 pointing back at me, but you know Satan is behind it. All he wants is to be worshiped. He wants to deceive the entire world. When Jesus comes there will be no doubt that it is the Lord.

The world we live in is a powder keg, especially the Middle East, Israel, surrounded by countries that want to destroy them. We have had two world wars but not every nation was involved. In the end, every nation will be involved somehow. This is the first time since the creation of the world and man, and that means Satan had the power to destroy everything completely when Jesus was telling these four disciples what was going to transpire centuries from that point in time. Particularly with sophisticated weapons, nuclear power can blow this world apart, and as we move forward, we will see that it will be used.

The rise of the Antichrist will be one of the first events that we will see at the fast-approaching end of the age. It will be a time of terror for the entire world. It will be the condition of the world that makes this rise possible and will cause this terror. The Antichrist will be the one who resolves the issues and relieves the world of trouble. The Antichrist will be the one with all the answers. Daniel referred to the rise of the little horn. New and amazing engines of war will bring the world to a state of terror, and will have superior weapons so that he can single handedly destroy anything that comes against him. He will weld together the nations of Europe to form a new empire of vast wealth and power.

I'm going to insert here from my last book, the European German Chancellor from November, 2018 Radio Free Europe Angela Merkel is calling for the eventual creation of a european army reflecting the sentiments of French President Emmanuel Macron. What is really important in the value of the developments of the past year is that we have to work on a vision of one day creating a real army, Merkel noted in a speech before the European Parliament in Strasbourg on November 13th. A common european army would show the world that there will never again be war between the European countries. Merkel said this as she envisioned a European army that would function in parallel with NATO, and come under a European Security Council. "Europe must take our fate into our own hands, if we want to protect our community."

Merkel said these things a week after Macron called for a European army that would give Europe greater independence from the United States, as well as defend their continent against such possible aggressors as Russia and China. The Lord perked my ears up when I heard of this happening in 2018. Jesus said in Mark 13:33 (Living Bible) And since you don't know when that time will come, be on guard! and Stay Alert! I said to you what I say to everyone, watch for him.

There are talks about a 10-nation confederacy. Finland, in November of the same year, 2018, joined the European Union, which completed the 10-nation. Whether this is the 10-nation confederacy, only God knows. In both Daniel and Revelation, there is talk about the 10 nations, so this meeting in Strasburg was very significant, although it is in its embryonic state, saying that this European army is going to happen. Western Europe has the finances to build this massive army.

The European Union, located in Brussels, the old European common market, is on the move. When it amasses this army, a world leader will emerge - the Antichrist - with a religious guru by his side. These two have the full embodiment of Satan himself. The European Union has its own money system, and it says that the Antichrist and the false prophet will rule from Rome, the seven hills. At one time there was a ruler, a Roman emperor who was crowned by Pope Leo the 3rd at Saint Peter's Basilica in Rome. On December 25th, 800 this emperor's name was Charlemagne and his inscription is on the euro money system in the European Union. In addition, there is a building named after him at the European Union in Brussels. He was a talented diplomat, an administrator who ruled from Western Europe. Christ said that there will be wars and rumors of war and other commotions that Jesus mentioned. First. is the beginning of these things that coincide with the start of the tribulation. They come before the beginning of sorrows. Jesus said that when you see these things know that it is near, even at the door. Jesus had just said the end is not yet, and this is telling us that while the end is not yet, the following things must happen before the end comes.

I thought that we could focus on this, since we are in shutdown mode across the world and things are very bad, and I looked, and behold a pale horse, and his name that sat on him was death, and hell followed with him. Power was given unto them over a fourth part of the earth to kill with sword and with hunger and death, and with the beast of the earth. The rider is limited to a fourth part of the earth, probably the part which the Antichrist controls. The earthquakes are described in Revelation. People realize that these judgments are coming from He who sits on the throne. These are the beginning of sorrows, wars, strife, famine, and pestilence on earth. Falling stars seem bad enough, but they are only the beginning. The Antichrist attempts to rid the earth of christians. Jesus adds the details that they will be hated of all nations. Many will betray one another and the false prophets will deceive many. It's going to be a strange situation. Wars will break out everywhere, riots, strikes, commerce paralyzed, just like it is today. Around the world people will be starving. People panic-buying, hoarding, pests and wild animals, stars falling to earth.

You would think these rulers would have something more to think about than those being converted to christianity, but Satan, the one leading, has been nonstop against this revival. Revelation 6:15 through 17(NKJ) says And the kings of the earth, the great men, the rich men, the commanders, and the mighty, men and every slave and every free man hid themselves in the dens and in the rocks of the mountains, and said "Fall on us and hide us from the face of He that sits on the throne, and from the wrath of the Lamb! For the great day of his wrath has come, and who shall be able to stand? Kings and great men? Know that God's Judgment has come.

I'm going to make a right turn here in my all-terrain vehicle, and head back to 9/11, 2001, when Islamic terrorists hit America. I could ask each and every one of you what you were doing that day when the Lord woke up America, and the world flew commercial airplanes into New York. These flying bombs first hit the north tower, then as we watched this nightmare unfold another plane hit the South tower, and we saw a huge fireball coming out on the other side of the building. That day is etched in all of our minds, as we watched these two buildings collapse. When I recall other events, there hasn't been anything that has stood out in my memory, except the Kennedy assassination, the Apollo flights, and the man on the moon, that has made its way to the front of my mind.

Alexander Graham Bell was born March 3rd, 1847. He was Scottish born and died August 2nd, 1922. He was an american inventor, scientist and engineer, and is credited with inventing and patenting the first practical telephone. He also co-founded the American Telephone and Telegraph company around 1874. Where, with that first call through the wire to Watson, he also invented the hearing aid. Could you imagine what he would think if he could see what is happening 146 years later? Look at social media today, plus everything that comes from the telephone and telecommunication. Everything is affected by these two inventions.

Then you can look at the first powered aircraft on December 17th, 1903, when Wilbur and Orville Wright made four brief flights at Kitty Hawk North Carolina. The Wright brothers had invented the first successful airplane flight. We can look at travel today. As of August 5th, 2016 the heaviest air traffic day that was recorded was 12,856 flights, and over 1,590,929 people were in the sky at the same time (source at FlightAware). From the Wright brothers from Kitty Hawk to where we are today, when they now want to travel to Mars. There are companies involved. Richard Branson at Virgin Airways wants to develop domestic flights that leave the earth atmosphere in space, and re-enter somewhere else around the world within minutes. Amazing! So as Jesus said, having this discourse with the four disciples, he knew the events that he told them about in Matthew, Mark and Luke. He knew about the Book of Revelation, and that one of the four disciples which we discussed was John, of the inner circle, of Jesus, along with Peter and James. John was in exile on the island of Patmos when Jesus' revelation was unveiled to him. We see in Matthew 4:1(Living Bible) Then Jesus was led by the Spirit into the wilderness to be tempted there by the devil . For forty days and forty nights.he fasted and became very hungry.

and Satan attacked the Lord. He always combated the enemy with the Word of God, and that's how we combat him also.

I want to focus on when the Devil took him to the peak of a very high mountain, and showed him all the kingdoms of the world in their glory. I will give it all to you, he said, if you would kneel down and worship me. There it is! He wants to be worshiped and he will give all his power to these two men, the Antichrist and the false prophet. In verse 10, Jesus said, get out of here Satan, for the scripture says you must worship the Lord your God and serve only him. In John 8:44,(Living Bible) Jesus told these so-called religious leaders, for you are the children of your father the devil and you love to do the evil things he does. He was a murderer from the beginning. He has always hated the truth, because there is no truth in him. When he lies it is consistent with his character, for he is a liar and the father of lies. So, as we look at Matthew 25 and Mark 13 when Jesus replied, don't let anyone mislead you for many will come in my name claiming I am the Messiah, we can see that Satan is behind it. All of you will hear of wars and threats of wars.

Just yesterday the United States intelligence got word that Iran had plans to attack our troops in Iraq, so president Trump sent a stern warning to the leaders of Iran in the middle of this pandemic crisis. There will be earthquakes in many parts of the world. I say this because within the last week here in the U.S., in Utah and the neighboring state of Idaho, there were earthquakes.

From this point, I want to ride over the rough terrain of Matthew 24, and head down the valley of Matthew 25, where Jesus gives this parable. have been looking for his coming. Jesus said, then the Kingdom of Heaven will be like ten bridesmaids who took their lamps and went out to meet the bridegroom (which is Jesus). Five of them were wise and five were foolish. Those who were foolish took their lamps and took no oil with them. Oil is a symbol of the Holy Spirit. But the wise took oil with their lamps. While the bridegroom was delayed, they all slumbered, and at midnight a cry was heard. Behold! The bridegroom is coming out to meet him! All the virgins rose and trimmed their lamps, and the foolish said to the wise, give us some of your oil, for our lamps are going out. But the wise answered no, lest there should not be enough for us, but go rather to those who buy and sell for yourselves. While they went to buy oil, the bridegroom came and those who were ready went in with him to the wedding, and the door was shut afterwards. The other virgins came also saying Lord, open to us, but he answered, assuredly I say to you, I do not know you. Watch, therefore, for you know neither the day nor the hour in which the Son of Man is coming.

I now have to move up the terrain of God's Word, then make communication with the captain of the Lord's army, our Lord and Savior, Jesus Christ, to get my reconnaissance (military observation of a region to locate an enemy, in this case, Satan). There are many symbols in the Book of Revelation, and we're on a mission with the leading Holy Spirit to decode these symbols, and the underlying message that our Lord is revealing to us. But at the beginning of Revelation there is a blessing to those who read and obey it. Christ's return will change things on earth and he will return in the clouds Acts 1:6-11(LivingBible) When the apostles were with Jesus, they kept asking him, Lord, has the time come for you to free Israel and restore our Kingdom? He replied that the Father alone has the authority to set those dates and times, and they are not for you to know. You will receive power when the Holy Spirit comes upon you, and you will be my witnesses, telling people about me everywhere in Jerusalem, throughout Judea and Samaria, and to the ends of the earth. After saying this, he was taken up into the clouds while they were watching, and they could no longer see him. As they strained to see him rising into heaven, two men in white robes suddenly stood among them. Men of Galilee, they said, why are you standing here staring into heaven? Jesus has been taken from you into Heaven, but someday he will return from Heaven the same way you saw him go!

Now let's head back to Jerusalem through the Arabian desert on the east side of Israel, and out to where the Euphrates and Tigris rivers are drying up to make a way for the kings of the east. This is a massive army of 200,000,000. When I looked this up, I found that the Euphrates River is mentioned in the Book of Revelation, in a prophecy that is predicted to occur just before Jesus returns at the end of the great tribulation, and when the global destruction in the last days is threatening the very existence of life on earth (Revelation 16:12)(LivingBible) Then the great Euphrates and Tigris Rivers dried up, and NASA studies recently have indicated that the fertile region in the Middle East is losing fresh water at a rapid rate. The water flow in the important Euphrates and Tigris Rivers has decreased as a result of this trend, and formerly arable land in the area has become cracked and dry.

During their upcoming battles of World War III, just before the attack by China and other countries to the east, upon Israel. The Euphrates will be removed as an obstacle, having been dried up. This permits the march of a 200,000,000-man army to the valley of Jehoshaphat (Megiddo), to the battle of Armageddon, just as Christ returns to fight them (Revelation 9:16)(NKJ) There won't be any fight, but could the current trend toward the drought in this region, and the dramatic decrease in the Tigris and the Euphrates Rivers in recent years, be the first stage of the fulfillment of this prophecy? It appears that this is just another important indication of how close we are to the second coming! We can no longer put our fingers in our ears and go "la la la, I don't want to hear about the end times."

The Trumpet.com refers to the first meeting marked the first time India and Pakistan participated as full members. Both became full members last year, adding their large population and nuclear armed militaries to the bloc. Yet the true powers of the SCO (Shanghai Cooperation Organization). are still China and Russia. The Chinese Minister of National Defense, General Wei Feng, presided over the summit and delivered a keynote speech. The

Shanghai spirit should be well preserved, he said, while pragmatic cooperation is strengthened in areas such as high-level exchanges, joint military drills and education, among others.

The strengthening of cooperation between these eight Asian nations is deeply significant in light of Bible prophecies for modern day Asia. We know that this is not going to happen. Russia is not going to be in this coalition with China. God has another plan for Russia. We can see in Ezekiel 38-39 that God is going to put a hook into Russia's jaw. It says that if you draw a straight line from the far north of Israel it runs into Russia (referred to in the Bible as Gog). It says that they are in league with these Muslim nations. It says that a massive army will be led by Russia, and that they will march down through the mountains of Israel and meet their fate by the hand of God. When they enter Israel, they will be destroyed. In addition, in 1965 China proclaimed they could man this exact number of 200,000,000 men. It will be as God's Word says, kings of the East joining with China.

Around AD 96, the apostle John recorded a striking prophecy about a military force that would emerge in the end times, "And the number of the army of the horseman were two hundred thousand-thousand, and I heard the number of them (Revelation 9:16)). This is describing a military force of 200 million. This jaw dropping number is a magnitude larger than the largest army in human history. The jaw drops further when we consider how many people were alive when John recorded this prophecy. The estimated number of the population on the planet was around 150 million. This is compelling evidence that this prophecy is for this modern age. Only in recent times have national populations swelled large enough to make a military force of this size even possible. Yet, even in this modern era of a population explosion such an army is enormous. Where could this many troops come from?

Historical data shows that nations can field roughly one fighting man for every 15 adults in a population, and in extremes, 1 in 10 adults could be made soldiers. In the United States today, there are 332,278,200 250 million adults. That means in a time of extreme measures we could possibly man an army of around 25 million troops (this is more than 15 times the current number). By this formula, The European Union's vast population could field a force of around 40 million, the combined countries of Latin America could produce an army of 48 million, those of Africa, 70 million. These impressive figures are still a far cry from the 200-million-man force that the Revelation 9:16 prophecies say will rise up in the end times. It is only from a combination of Asian nations that an army of this enormous size could be assembled. The combined population of the SCO member states is 3.2 billion, of which 25 billion are adults. Even if we go with the low end of the formula, building a military of 200 million men from these Asian nations is demographically feasible. It should come as no surprise then, that in Revelation 16:12 John refers to this 200-million-man army as the kings of the east. This incomparably huge force will be a confederacy of several Asian nations. The Trumpet.Com has said for years that these kings of the east will be some of the main players in a nuclear World War III, and that they will be led by China. China is the regional behemoth driving the assembling of these eastern nations, and the S.C.O. may prove to be the vehicle they use to achieve that goal. To understand the significance of a united Asian bloc and how it is connected to the most inspiring event that the earth has ever seen.

Chapter 3

Turning Back the Pages of Time:

We are going to head north to Thessalonica and dig into the writings of Paul, but first I want to make a stop at Jeremiah 1:5(LivingBible) which states, *I knew you before I formed you in your mother's womb. I set you apart and appointed you as my prophet to the nations.* That's every one of us. *Jeremiah 17:9-10 (Living Bible) says, the human heart is deceitful above all things and desperately wicked. Who really knows how bad it is? But I the Lord search all hearts and examine secret motives. I give all people their due rewards, according to what their actions deserve.* Now, let's dig into God's Word from the Archives of Jeremiah. So, bring your shovel, as we are going on an expedition to reach the hidden treasures of this Book. God gave His people, Jerusalem and Judah, a warning. Maybe He is giving us a warning too! Let's grab our map {God's Word} and venture forth. Let's look at a time when Israel and Judah turned away from the Lord. When Josiah tore down the idols that Jeroboam had built which caused Israel to sin, Josiah demolished the shrines and killed the priest of these pagan gods (the bottom line of which is that Satan is behind it all, causing the evil that made Israel and Judah to sin).

A Chinese man moved to the United States. He went back to China to visit a friend and asked him if there were any idol worshippers there. The friend responded that there were idol worshippers. In the winter they worship a little fat man with a beard dressed in a red suit. In the spring they worship an easter bunny and in the fall, they worship a turkey. You might say oh, come on, that's a little far-fetched. Is it really? Let's look at the commercialism surrounding Christmas and Easter Sunday. The Lord is lost in both of these holidays. One atheist got a nativity scene in the public park taken down, and they are trying to get songs taken off the radio that mention the Lord, like Silent Night and O' Holy Night. They want to only play Frosty the Snowman, Here comes Santa Claus, and Jingle Bells. They are fun songs, but really where are we heading, taking Christ out of Christmas, and saying Merry Xmas? It is exactly what the Lord said would happen prior to His return - that it will get worse and worse. Everyone reading this can see the world we are living in, and see the decay of this world.

Now we go back to Jeremiah 3:6-25 when the Lord spoke to Jeremiah and said, *return to me*, but Israel did not turn back. Israel and Judah turned away and continued in their sins. The Lord wanted to forgive them and heal them, for they had forgotten the Lord their God. God said, *turn away from sin and return to me. I will put away your abomination (sins) out of my sight.* In Romans 3:23(NKJ) *for all have sinned and fall short of the glory of God.* In 1 John 1:9, if we confess our sins to him, he is faithful and just to forgive our sins. In Micah 7:19(LivingBible *Once again you will have compassion on us. You will trample our sins under your feet. You can throw them into the depths of the ocean.*

The underlying message of the Lord pertinent to us today. God wants to forgive us, if we would but give our lives to him and lean on him to guide us through our lives. In Prov. 3-5(NKJ) *Trust in the Lord with all your heart and lean not on your own understanding. In all your ways acknowledge Him and he will direct your path* (Jeremiah 4:31). Israel, if you want to return to me, plow up the hard ground of your hearts. God is warning Israel and Judah that trouble is coming. They have turned their hearts from the Lord just like the world we live in today. The Lord told Jeremiah that our enemy rushes down upon us like storm clouds. As the Lord warned Judah and Jerusalem how terrible it will be, so we are doomed. Cleanse your hearts. Your destruction has been announced, just as He warns us of the end times. This is what the Lord says, and He warned Jerusalem and Judah. He is warning the world of what is coming. The entire land will be ruined, but I will not destroy it completely (v.28). The earth will mourn and the heavens will be draped in black. We have turned away from the Lord. I have made up my mind and will not change it. This is it finalized! In Ephesians 1:12 first, we have to praise and glorify him for what He has done for us and what Jesus did for us on the cross (v.7). He is so rich in kindness and *Grace* that he purchased our freedom with the blood of his son and forgave our sins. In John 14:1-5(LivingBible) Jesus was explaining to his disciples that he will be leaving to prepare a place for them and us too. Jesus said I will come and get you so that you will always be with me wherever I am, and you know the way to where I'm going. Then Thomas, being real, said to Jesus no, we don't know. We have no idea where you are going so how can we know the way? Then Jesus gave one of the greatest scripture verses in all the Bible (v.6), I am the way the truth and the life no one can come to the Father except through me. That's it! We cannot work our way to heaven. We only get there by what Christ did for us on the cross. He gave his life for us. In Romans, 10:9-10, if we openly declare that Jesus is Lord and believe in our heart that God raised him from the dead, you will be saved, (Verse 13) for everyone who calls on the name of the Lord shall be saved.

Chapter 4

In search of the archives of Paul's writing:

We will head up to Tyre and catch a boat ride to Thessalonica to search Paul's writings in verses 1 and 2. In Thessalonians 1:10, they speak of how you are looking forward to the coming of God's Son from Heaven. Jesus, whom God raised from the dead, is the one who rescued us from the terrors of coming judgments. Our purpose is to please God, not people, and he alone examines the motives of our hearts (4:14). For since we believe that Jesus died and was raised to life again, we also believe that when Jesus returns, he'll bring back the believers who have died.

In Revelation 19:11(LivingBible), Then I saw heaven opened and a white horse standing there. Its rider was named Faithful and True (Jesus), and so he judges fairly and wages righteous war. His eyes were like flames of fire and on his head were many crowns. A name was written on him no one understood except himself. He wore a robe dipped in blood and His title was the Word of God. The armies of Heaven, dressed in the finest of pure white linen, followed him on white horses. If you are a believer in Christ, that is us in this army. From his mouth came a sharp sword to strike down the Nations. He will rule them with an iron rod, and He will release the fierce wrath of God the Almighty, like juice flowing from a wine press.

On His robe at His thigh was *written* this title, King of Kings and Lord of Lords. Then I saw an angel standing in the sun, shouting to the vultures flying high in the sky. Come and eat the flesh of kings, generals and strong warriors of horses and their riders, and of all humanity both free and slave, small and great.

This next picture John is giving us is a picture at the beginning of this book. When we jumped into the stealth, sand rail went up through the mountains of Israel, to the valley of Megiddo and the Battle of Armageddon. Now we're seeing it from a bird's eye view, with the Lord on horseback, and we are following with Him. Then John said, I saw the beast (Antichrist) and the kings of the world, with their armies gathered together to fight against the One sitting on the horse and His army (if you know Christ as your Savior we are in that army). The beast was captured and with him the false prophet, who performed mighty miracles on behalf of the beast. These miracles deceived all who accepted the mark of the beast and his false prophet (The Antichrist and religious guru) and all who worshiped his statue. Both the Beast and the false prophet were thrown alive into the fiery lake of burning sulfur. Their entire army was killed by the sharp sword that came from the mouth of the one riding the white horse, and the vultures all gorged themselves on the dead bodies. I watched the Ten Commandments the other day, and I was so impressed with how Cecil B. DeMille captured this Biblical and epic event, but no one could capture what John saw as he was put forth into this future event.

We now head back to 1st Thessalonians 4:15(LivingBible) where we have the rapture of the Church. We tell you this directly from the Lord: we who are still living when the Lord returns will not meet him ahead of those who have died. For the Lord Himself will come down from Heaven with a commanding shout, with the voice of the archangel and with the trumpet call of God. First, the believers who have died will rise from their graves. Then, together with them, we who are still alive and remain on the earth will be caught up in the clouds to meet the Lord. We will then be with the Lord forever, so encouraging each other with these words is important.

In 5:9, For God chose to save us through our Lord Jesus Christ, not to pour out his anger on us. 2 Thessalonians 1:7, He will come with his mighty angels in flaming fire, bringing judgement on those who do not love God and those who refused to obey the Good News of our Lord Jesus. They will be punished with eternal destruction, forever separated from the Lord and from his glorious power. 2:3 says, don't be fooled by what they say, for that day will not come until there is a great rebellion against God and the lawless one is revealed – the one who brings destruction. He will exalt himself and defy everything that people call god, and every object of worship. He will even sit in the temple of God, claiming that he himself is God (this is the abomination of desolation).

Don't you remember that I told you about all of this when I was with you? You know what is holding him back, for He can only be revealed when His time comes. This lawlessness is already secretly at work, and it will remain secret until the one who was holding him back steps out of the way (The Holy Spirit). The man of lawlessness will then be revealed. The Lord Jesus will kill him with the breath of His mouth, and will destroy him by the splendor of His coming. This man will come to do the work of Satan with counterfeit power and signs and so-called miracles. He will use every kind of evil deception to fool those on their way to destruction, because they refuse to love and accept the truth that would save them. As a result, God will cause them to be greatly deceived, and they will believe these lies, and they will be condemned for enjoying evil rather than believing the truth. We have to remember the Lord our God is still in control of everything that is going to transpire. But the Lord is faithful, and He will strengthen you and guard you from the evil one.

Chapter 5

Who Is the Antichrist?

Some say that he is alive today, somewhere in the world (Revelation 13:1-4).(Living Bible) He is referred to as a beast. Revelation 13:1(Living Bible) Then I saw a beast rising up out of the sea.

Revelation depicts the Antichrist as a beast on 32 separate occasions. The image points to the brutal and bloody, uncontrolled and wild character of this diabolical dictator. It also contrasts the Antichrist with Christ, who is most commonly called the Lamb. The Lamb saves sinners but the Beast ferociously persecutes and executes the saints. The Lamb is loving but the Beast is heartless and cruel. The Beast Rises out of the sea. The sea refers to the Gentile Nations (Revelation 17:15), LivingBible)Then the angel said to me "The waters where the prostitute is ruling represents masses of people of every7 nation and language indicating that the Antichrist will be a gentile. Anti can mean instead of, against or opposed to, so the Antichrist is against Christ, opposed to Christ.

The Antichrist is the man of lawlessness, the son of destruction who will lead the world into rebellion against God (2 Thessalonians 2:9-11(, This man will come to do the work of Satan with counterfeit power and signs and miracles. He will use every kind of evil deception to fool those on their way to destruction. because they refuse to love and accept the truth that would save them. So God will cause them to be greatly deceived. Revelations 11:7), and deceive the multitudes (Revelation 19:20). He has great power with 10 horns and 7 heads (13:1). We see this because animals use horns for battle, which is a symbol of power, and the Dominion represents kingdoms and kings.

Comparing this text to Daniel 7:16-24, we can conclude that the Antichrist will rise up from the ten kingdoms that will constitute a revived Roman Empire, the final form of gentile world power before Christ returns. Some Bible expositors say that the seven heads are the principal rulers of the Antichrist revived Roman Empire. Others suggest that the seven heads may be successive World Empires (Revelations 17:9). A mountain can symbolize a kingdom (Daniel 12:34-45). This may be a veiled reference to Rome, which was built on Seven Hills (Revelation 17:18). All of these views support the idea that the kingdom of the Antichrist will be a revived Roman Empire, a global power with ten diadems on its horns (a ten-nation confederacy). The 10 diadems, or crowns, point to the domination of the Antichrist kingdom, which will eventually embrace the entire globe. There will be blasphemous names on his head (13:1). (LivingBible) This points to the character of the Antichrist. His mouth will be full of blasphemy (Revelation 13:5-6)(Living Bible) And he will exalt himself above all that is called God or that is worshiped (2 Thessalonians 2:4).(Living Bible)

There will be a great army. The Beast was like a leopard (13:2). (LivingBible) Much of the imagery in this verse is from Daniel. The leopard was known for its swiftness, cunning and agility (Daniel 7:6).(Living Bible) This imagery in Daniel represents Greece under Alexander the Great, which was a swift, cunning and agile army. Such will be the case with the Antichrist as he comes into world domination. Its feet were fierce like that of a bear. The bear in

Daniel's account refers to the Medo-Persia empire (Daniel 7:5), well known for its strength and fierceness in battle Isaiah (13:17-18).

Such strength and fierceness will certainly characterize the Antichrist and his forces. Its mouth was like iron. The lion in Daniel refers to Babylon (Daniel 7:4). With lion-like qualities of power and strength, Babylon was known for its ability to move quickly (like a lion). Such qualities will also characterize the Antichrist. The Antichrist will be severely wounded,Revelation 13:14(Living Bible) It says, Satan will supernaturally heal this wound. Perhaps he will only appear to have been killed, though he really has not, and through satanic trickery he will appear to be resurrected. Remember that Satan can only duplicate, he cannot create.

From our studies we know that Satan wants to be worshiped. Remember that this is his answer to the Trinity, that Satan is in the place of God. The Antichrist taking the place of Jesus. This is his answer to the resurrection of Christ, a great deception that will deceive the whole world into following the Antichrist more than before. Satan has supernatural abilities, but he is not powerful enough to raise people from the dead. Only God can create life. With his vast knowledge Satan is a master magician and a super scientist. With his vast knowledge of God and man and the universe, he is able to perform counterfeit miracles (2 Thessalonians 2:9)(Living Bible). This man will come to do the work of Satan with counterfeit power, signs and miracles. He will use every kind evil deception to fool those on their way to destruction (2 Corinthians 4:4).(LivingBible)

Satan, who is the god of this world, has blinded the minds of those who do not believe. They are unable to see the glorious light of the Good News (God's Word). They do not understand this message about the glory of Christ, who is in the exact likeness of God. The Antichrist receives his orders and strategy from Satan. He will ravage this world with hellish ferocity in order to establish complete domination over this awestruck earth. The entire earth marveled as they followed the Beast and pledged their allegiance (Revelation 13:3).(Living Bible) This event will no doubt make headlines around the world. Internet videos of this event will go viral. Television reports of this event will be shown around the clock.

Before he was Satan, he was known as Lucifer. Let's read what Isaiah said in 14:12-17(Living **Bible)**. How you are fallen from heaven O shining star son of the morning! You have been thrown down to the earth, you who destroyed the nations of the world. For you said to yourself, I will ascend to heaven and set my throne above God's Stars. I will proceed to the mountain of the gods far away in the north. I will climb to the highest heavens and be the most-high. Instead, you will be brought down to the place of the dead, down to the lowest depths. Everyone there will stare at you and ask can this be the one who shook the earth and made the kingdoms of the world tremble? Is this the one who destroyed the world and made it into a wasteland?

We can look at The Archives of World War II and see how Hitler, as one man, deceived a whole nation. It said that Hitler was a Satan worshipper. It fits in the way that he drove the masses to hysteria with his messages to the German people, and the evil killing of over 6 million Jews. It definitely was as if he was possessed when he spoke, but that will be like child's play when the Antichrist comes to power. He will deceive the whole world. The judgment of mankind is coming like a roaring train, speeding to its final destination.

As we look at God's Word, we can see the character of the Antichrist. Jesus said if those days are not shortened, there would not be anyone who would survive. The Antichrist has more than military, political and economic savvy. In fact, he is directly connected {possessed) by the god of this present world at his disposal. The Lord Jesus will overthrow this Lawless one with the breath of his mouth.

The depravity of this world is a cesspool. Here in America, we are still killing unborn babies at the rate of nearly 4,000 a day. There is Godless porn, violence in ideology, and any media they can get their hands on. We are so divided in this country, and the hatred is rampant. France is seeking to lower the age of sexual consent to 13. Australia is about to vote on same-sex marriage and over 60% are okay with it, just like here in the U.S. and worldwide. We can see the depravity in this world now and how bad it's going to become, and we can see that in the middle of it is Satan - stirring the pot.

The Apostle Paul made it clear that one of the most important signs of the last days would be that men would succeed in taking God out of their lives (Isaiah 13:9-11-13 (Living Bible) For see the day of the Lord is coming, the Terrible Day of His Fury and fierce anger. The Lord will punish the world for its evil and the wicked for their sin. This is why we have to look at Mark 13:23. Watch Out! I have warned you about this ahead of time!

`Let's hit the pause button, pull up on the side of the road overlooking the Aegean Sea, and reflect on God's Word. Jesus said in Matthew 16:2(LivingBible) You know the saying red sky at night means fair weather tomorrow, "red sky in the morning means foul weather all day. You know how to interpret the weather signs in the sky but you do not know how to interpret the signs of the times! There it is! Here we are April 10th 2020, Good Friday, and things are still the same - shut down due to the Coronavirus pandemic. But there is one thing that does not change - what God did for us when He gave the world His son. This is what Jesus did for us on the cross. He gave his life for our sins, and through his death we can have eternal life if we accept him as our savior. He took our place, as we deserve death. Then Sunday came, and Jesus defeated Satan and death when He rose in all his glory. Thank you, Lord, for what you did for us.

Let us now look at what Hal Lindsey says in an article he wrote called Last Day Warnings. I've been studying his writings for 45 years. He has devoted his life to the study of End Time Prophecy. As the world reels under the impact of the latest Middle East crisis, and I guess we can add this worldwide pandemic, many are discovering that these events are fitting into larger, precisely predicted events. The pattern is to be found woven throughout the Hebrew Prophets, from Moses to Jesus Christ and John the apostle. The prophecies were made over a period of 3500 years. Throughout these predictions, it is clear that these events are to lead to the final seven-year period of world catastrophe. This climax will consist of a global war of such great magnitude, that only the personal and visible return of Jesus Christ to this earth will save man from self-annihilation.

Things we are seeing: Listed are 20 pieces of this pattern which are unmistakably coming together for the first time in history.

1. The return of the dispersed Jews to become a nation again in 1948.
2. The Jews recaptured the old city of Jerusalem in the 1967 Arab Israeli War.
3. The rise of Russia as a powerful nation and enemy of Israel.
4. The Arab Confederation against the new state of Israel.
5. The rise of a military power in the Orient that can field an army of 200 million soldiers. Red China alone boasts that they can man an army of this proportion.
6. The revival of the old Roman Empire in the Form a 10-Nation Confederacy, believed to be the European union (the old European common market), will ultimately be this power.
7. The revival of the dark occultic practices of ancient Babylon.
8. The unprecedented turn to drugs.

9. The increase in international revolution.
10. The increase in the number of wars.
11. The increase in the number of earthquakes.
12. The increase in famine through the population explosion.
13. The surge in plagues.
14. The increasing pollution.
15. The departure of many christian churches from the historic truth of christianity.
16. The move toward a one world religion.
17. The move to one world government.
18. The decline of the United States as a major world power.
19. The increase in lawlessness.
20. The decline of the family unit.

Things To Watch: The Arabs will continue to bring great pressure upon the western nations to support their demands against Israel. They will do so through the continued restriction of oil without which the industrial nations cannot survive. They may begin to use their vast financial power to seriously threaten the economy of the United States as well. It is doubtful that Fort Knox could back up the dollars they hold if they demand gold for them. The United States will see some severe economic shocks resulting from the European Union and the Arab oil squeeze, and will continue to decline as the major power due to these shocks, as well as internal decay! The European Union will begin to emerge as the greatest economic power in history. Israel will continue to increasingly become the Western world's dilemma. The Middle East will continue to be the most dangerous threat to world peace in history.

The prophets clearly say that the spark that will set off Armageddon will be struck by the invasion of Israel by the Russian-led Arab coalition of nations against Israel. Jesus predicted these days in which we are currently living, when he said that when you see these things, know that He is at the door and ready to return. Then He said that this generation will not pass away until all of this is fulfilled. Matthew 24-32(Living Bible) says that we should now learn a lesson from the fig tree, that when its branches bud and its leaves begin to sprout you know that summer is near. In the same way, when you see all these things you can know his return is very near.

Could Israel in 1948 be the sign of the fig tree budding forth? According to Siri, a generation is 40-70 or 100 years. 40 and 70 years have come and gone. Only God knows, but verse 44(Living Bible) says it all - you also must be ready all the time for the Son of Man will come when least expected.

Because we are seeing all of these signs that fit into the predicted pattern, maybe we are the generation that will see the culmination of these prophecies, and the return of Christ. Who knows, perhaps this will be the year of Christ's sudden and mysterious Coming, to snatch out all those who believe in him. Again, only God knows! For thus saith the Lord of host, yet once it is a little while, and I will shake the heavens and the earth and the sea and the dry land; and I will shake all nations and the desire of all nations shall come; and I will fill this temple with glory, saith the Lord of hosts (Hag 2:6-7).(NKNJ)

Matthew 24:27(NKJ) says, For as the lightning comes out of the east and flashes to the the west, so shall also will the coming of the Son of Man upon the earth. The stress of nations with perplexity (literally means no way out), the sea and the waves roaring, and nations may fight among themselves. This is exactly what is going to happen. Throughout the reign of the Antichrist (after the rapture) there will be wars and strife, and peace will be taken from the earth. Nation will rise against nation at the coming of Christ. These nations will unite and send their armies to Jerusalem. The prophecy says that have I set my king upon my holy hill of Zion. The seas and waves could have two applications, could mean turbulent times. But we read in the scriptures that there will be great earthquakes that will move mountains into the sea. Such earthquakes could cause massive tidal waves, like the ones we have seen in the last few years, when it is said that an earthquake of a magnitude over 9 struck out in the Indian Ocean, and caused a massive tsunami that we all witnessed on TV. Also, another massive earthquake hit off the coast of Japan and caused another tsunami. I felt the power of some earthquakes as I was growing up in Southern California and I thought they were strong. It gets your attention very quickly. That rolling of the earth beneath you stops you in your tracks, because you don't know how intense it will be or how long it will last.

But in the end of time, the Lord is going to shake the earth to the point that it actually moves the earth's axis. No one could imagine that power. Revelation 16:18-20 says, and there was a great earthquake, such as was not since man has been on the Earth, so mighty an earthquake and so great. Every island fled away and mountains will not be found. Every island will be swallowed up and every mountain leveled.

Chapter 6

Continuing Our Journey for God's hidden Truths:

Let's catch a flight over to 1st and 2nd Timothy. This is good and pleases God our Savior, who wants everyone to be saved and understand the truth. 1st Timothy 6:15-16(Living Bible) says that At just the right time, Christ will be revealed from heaven by the blessed and only almighty God, the King of all Kings and the Lord of all lords. He alone can never die and he lives in a light so brilliant that no human can approach him. No human eye has ever seen him nor ever will. All honor and power to him forever! Amen. 11 Timothy 1:7(LivingBible) says, For God has never given us a spirit of fear and timidity but of power and love and self-discipline (2:3),Endure suffering along with me as good soldiers of Christ Jesus. Soldiers do not get tied up in the affairs of civilian life, for they cannot please the officer who enlisted them.

2 Timothy 2:19(Living Bible) says, But God's truth stands firm like a foundation stone, with this inscription: the Lord knows those who are His and all who belong to the Lord must turn away from evil. 2 Timothy 3:1(Living Bible) says, You should know this Timothy, that in the last days there will be very difficult times. For people will love only themselves and their money. They will be

boastful and proud, scoffing of God, disobedient to their parents and ungrateful. They will consider nothing sacred. They will be unloving and unforgiving; they will slander others and have no self-control. They will be cruel and hate what is good. They will betray their friends, be reckless and puffed up with pride, and love pleasure rather than God. They will act religious, but they will reject the power that could make them Godly. Stay away from people like that. Verse 7 says that they are never able to understand the truth. Verse 8 says that they have depraved minds and counterfeit faith. 2 Timothy 4:5(Living Bible) says that Paul wrote this last letter to Timothy, do not be afraid of suffering for the Lord's work, and fully carry out the ministry God has given. Verses 6-7 state that Paul was about to be beheaded by Nero when he penned these words. The time of my death is near. I fought the good fight. I have finished the race and I remained faithful.

In John, chapter 6, are some other writings by this man. Let's set sail over to Ephesus, and dig deep into God's Word and The Archives of John, when he wrote the first, second, and third epistles of John. John was termed John the Evangelist, not John the Apostle, who wrote the Book of John. John wrote his writings later in life, as he really reflected on his life with the Savior around A.D 90 to 95.

John sat with Jesus, Jesus, James, Peter, and Andrew, before Jesus was crucified on the Mount of Olives. Jesus told these four disciples (Matthew 24:4-5(Living Bible) that many will come in My name claiming "I am the Messiah". They will deceive many. As we look at 1 John 2:18(Living Bible) that says, dear children, the last hour is here. You have heard that the antichrist is coming and already many such antichrists have appeared. He's talking about man. But to all who have rejected Jesus as their Savior, they are antichrists. Such teachers were spreading heresy. We are spreading false doctrine. 1 John 2:24(Living Bible) says, You must remain faithful to what you have been taught from the beginning. If you do, you will remain in fellowship with the Son and with the Father, and in this fellowship we enjoy the eternal life he promised us.

I am writing these things to warn you about those who want to lead you astray, but you have received the Holy Spirit and he lives within you, so, you don't need anyone to teach you what is true, it's not a lie. Just as he has taught you to remain in fellowship with Christ, 2 John I says this because many deceivers have gone out into the world. They deny that Jesus Christ came in a real body. Such a person is a deceiver and an antichrist, so watch out that you do not lose what you have worked so hard to achieve. Be diligent so that you receive your full reward. Anyone who wanders away from this teaching has no relationship with God, but anyone who remains in the teaching of Christ has a relationship with both the Father and the Son.

From this point let's take our compass and set sail heading southeast, back to Tyre, get on the stealth rider and head along the Sea of Galilee. We will go back to Jerusalem to the Mount of Olives, and move on to our final destination - the last paragraph of Revelation. Before that, we will listen in on the conversation in which Jesus was teaching the four disciples, as He is also teaching us. Yesterday was Easter, the same as that first Easter morning. You are the hope for all mankind, as You were the first light on that Easter, you are light today, Master. Psalm 125:2(Living Bible) says, Just as the mountains surround Jerusalem, so the Lord surrounds his people both now and forever. Psalm 120:1,(Living Bible) I took my troubles to the Lord. I cried out to him and he answered my prayer. Psalm 119:130(Living Bible), the teaching of your Word gives light, so that even the simple can understand. Psalm. 119:89(Living Bible) Your Word of the Lord stands firm in Heaven. Psalm 119:105(Living Bible) Your Word is the lamp to guide my feet and a light for my path. This one is something we all need to search for within our hearts. 119:2(Living Bible) joyful are those who obey his laws and search for him with all their heart. Psalm 118:1(Living Bible) Give thanks to the Lord for he is good. Psalm 118:15(Living Bible) The strong right arm of the Lord has done glorious things (that means power and strength). Psalm 118:22(Living Bible), The stone the builders rejected, has now become the cornerstone. Psalm 118:4 (Living Bible)This is the day the Lord has made we will rejoice and be glad in it. Psalm 118:27(Living Bible), The Lord is God shining upon us. Psalm 118:29(Living Bible), Give thanks to the Lord for he is good. His faithful love endures forever.

As we sit here today the death toll here in the United States has surpassed 70,000. I wonder how many knew you as their Savior Lord, or how many perished for the hardness of their hearts. According to our world, in data there is something more astonishing regarding how many people die in a one- year period around the world. This data from the year 2015 = 57 million. You take 365 days in a year, times 24 hours in a day, times 60 minutes in an hour, times 60 seconds in a minute, and you get 1.8 people dying every second, times 60 seconds, means 108 every minute. Multiply that by 60 minutes in an hour. That's 6,480. Then we take 6,480 times 24 hours in a day, and that's 155,520 in a day, times 365 days in a year =56,764,800. We come up a little short, but we get the idea. This is a statistic from 2015, so today's numbers are a lot higher. The bottom line is that we just don't know when our time is up.

I think my brother said it best. We are all in the waiting room. waiting for our number to be called. There is a lot of truth in this statement. Job 12:10 says, for the life of every living thing is in His hand, and the breath of every human being. Hebrews 9:27 (LivingBible) says that each person is destined to die once, and after that come's Judgment.

Lord, we have to stop and look at the events that have unfolded since this Coronavirus shut everything down. I know about social distancing. On Easter Sunday, a man was playing catch with his daughter and was arrested at a park. No one else was there. It was in Tennessee at a church worshiping you Lord in their cars and they were ticketing the cars. But this one Lord is something we have to stop and examine. They are talking about putting a chip on kids to keep track of vaccinating them, or giving them a credit card with a smart chip on them. Either way, Lord, it's interesting to watch this unfold. As I push through, Lord, on this journey up the terrain of your Word, I have to hit the pause button and look to where I'm heading on this expedition, pushing forward for the cross of Christ. As I am moving along in the Stealth Rider am I spinning my wheels, and I have to keep rolling to the Final Destination. I will not know until the end of this journey.

Let's move on and listen in with Jesus and the four disciples again. We have looked at the Antichrist, teaching wars and rumors of wars, famines, earthquakes. Jesus said these are only the beginning of birth pangs. I sometimes think I should have had a woman write this, because they know what the pain of birth is like. Jesus knows that He created this scenario. When a woman is in labor, the pain isn't as intense as just before birth. These signs Jesus is giving us are merely a build-up to Revelation. We've already touched on the fig tree. Jesus said that heaven and earth will disappear. God has prepared a new heaven and a new earth, and we will look closer at that in the Book of Revelation. He tells us that His word will never disappear. How does a man know if he is taking the right road? These are questions that I asked myself in my first book, and these are questions that I have to ask myself now. How do you know? You don't until this mission is over.

I have to go back to Proverbs, to one of my favorite Verses, 3:5-6. Trust in the Lord with all your heart, And lean not on your own understanding. In all your ways acknowledge Him and he will direct your path. There are three short stories I want to tell, then I will summarize them to fit my adventure. There was a boy, let's call him Johnny, who played baseball. His skill level was not that high. He was more of a two-inning player. The coach noticed that when his dad came to the game Johnny would grab hold of his hand or arm and point things out. Then the coach got word that Johnny's dad passed away. Johnny missed a few games before he returned to the team and when he returned, he went to the coach and asked if he could play that day. The coach felt badly for him and allowed him to play. That day, Johnny played a phenomenal game. He played as if he were a different kid. When the game was over, the coach went to Johnny as he was gathering his equipment together. The coach praised him for his playing, and Johnny thanked him and said, "I don't know if you knew that my dad was blind. You see coach, this is the first game my dad got to see me play."

The next story involves a mom who received a phone call from the school nurse saying that her daughter was extremely sick. She rushed to the school and took her daughter home. She put her in bed and hustled to the nearest drugstore. In her haste she locked her keys in the car. She purchased the medicine and the wire to get into the car. She rounded the wire to get into the car but was unsuccessful. She put her head against the car in frustration and prayed to the Lord for help. As she finished her prayer, a rough, scruffy man walked by, and she told him that she had locked her keys in the car and asked if he could help her. He walked over to the car, put the wire in the door and popped the lock within seconds. She said to him, "You're the answer to my prayers!" He said to her, "I don't know about that lady, I just got out of prison this morning."

The third story is about a six- year-old Sunday schooler. They were doing a study on the Book of Daniel when he was in the lion's den. The Sunday school teacher asked the question, "How do you think Daniel got saved from the lions? The little six-year-old responded that he had a lion from the tribe of Judah. Out of the mouths of babes!

The summarization of these three stories is this: When God calls your name to put you into the game of life, He will do it in a far different way from what you think, and the lion from the tribe of Judah will lead the way. Isaiah 6:8(Living Bible) says, Then I heard the Lord asking whom should I send as a messenger to this people? Who will go for us (what we have here is the Trinity)? God the Father was asking the question, and 'us', which is plural, means the Son and the Holy Spirit.

Lord, let me answer as Isaiah did. Here I am, send me. Proverbs:16-9(Living Bible) says that We can make our plans but the Lord determines our steps. Lord, keep leading my steps to the end of this journey. As it says in 1Thessalonians, The Day of the Lord will come like a thief in the night. A thief enters silently and unobtrusively, does his work and then is gone. Paul tells us that this is the way the Lord will come. The Air Force has a stealth bomber airplane, which is designed in such a way that it cannot be detected by radar. It can come upon an enemy unexpectedly and without warning. The Lord will come in the same way - like the stealth bomber - under the radar and unexpectedly. This is how the Day of the Lord begins.

I'm going to dig deeper into what the Lord said in the days of Noah. He said that people will be eating and drinking when suddenly the destructive judgment of God will fall upon them. As it says in Luke 17:26-28(NKJ, the world will be as in the days of Lot. People went about their daily business, eating and drinking, buying and selling, farming and building, until the morning Lot left Sodom. Then fire and burning sulfur rained down into the house. It says the same in Revelation about the Lake of Fire burning sulfur. Notice how clearly our Lord indicates in both of these examples that there will first be quiet disappearance of the family of God. In Matthew 24, the Olivet discourse says that two men will be working in the field and one will be taken and the other left. The parallel in Luke says that two men will be asleep in one bed, one will be taken and the other left. These examples occur during both day and night. This indicates that removal will happen simultaneously all over the earth. When it is day in one country and night in another, some will be taken and others left. Jesus then adds a clear and unmistakable warning to be watchful and ready, because the Son of Man will come at an hour when you do not expect him. "The Day of the Lord will also come suddenly with terrible and destructive judgment. The Day of the Lord would be a day of darkness and gloom, a day of clouds and blackness. Joel 2:2(LivingBible) says, a day of wrath, a day of distress and anguish, a day of trouble and ruin, a day of darkness and gloom. In Zephaniah 1:15, Jesus summed it up when he said the words, *then there will be a great distress unequaled from the beginning of the world until now, and never will be equaled again.*

The one thing that we must do is face exactly what God says is going to happen. The Day of the Lord is inevitable: These words from C.S. Lewis says that God is going to invade the earth in force, but what is the good of saying you are on his side when you see the entire natural universe melting away like a dream. Then something else, something that never entered your head, comes crashing in - something so beautiful to some of us and terrible to others - that none of us will have a choice. Prior to this time, it will be God without disguise; something so overwhelming that it will strike either irresistible love or irresistible horror into every creature. It will be too late then to choose your side. There is no use saying you choose to lie down after it has become impossible to stand up. That will not be the time for choosing. It will be the time when we discover which side we have really chosen, whether we realized it before or not. It will be the time when we discover which side we have really chosen, whether we realized it before or not.

Now, today at this moment, is our chance to choose the right side. God is holding back to give us that chance. It will not last forever. We must take it or leave it. If we trust in the Lord Jesus, if we have been born again by the Spirit, if we believe His Word and are growing by it, we are not destined for wrath but are guaranteed to escape from this terrible time of judgment. Just as Noah and Lot escaped the judgment that fell in their day, we will be with the Lord forever.

Our purpose for living is not to gain wealth and fame but to use our abilities and time to fulfill the will of God. We are to find the adventure of the ride with the Lord to His call and glorify Him. Revelation 1:8 (Living Bible)says, "I Am the Alpha and the Omega, the Beginning and the End. I am the one who is, who always was, and who is still to come - the Almighty One." Jesus speaks of his coming as unexpected and sudden, as a flood came upon the people of Noah's day. What was it about, this old man who was building this huge boat? People thought this old man was out of his mind. They didn't even know what rain was. God watered the earth from the ground, what was it that took billions to a watery grave? It is said that there were 7 to 10 billion people on the earth at the time. After the flood it took till the year 1804 to reach a billion. It took another hundred and twenty-three years to reach another billion in 1927; another 33 years to reach another billion in 1960; another 14 years in 1974 to reach another billion; another 13 years for another billion (5 billion), to where we are today in 2020, at 7-8 billion.

We see the heart of God. God's Spirit was grieved as he experienced sorrow. He is watching over us as a Father who feels our pain, and everything that we need. The bottom line is the days of Noah, the days of Lot, the days we live in today, and the days that are in the future. It goes back to the Garden of Eden with Adam and Eve, and there he is in the middle of the story - Satan. As Jesus said of this deceiver and liar, there is no truth in him, as we'll see whether we look at the story of Noah, or whether it's the days of Lot, or the morals of today's society, or the days were heading toward, with our foot full throttle to destruction.

As we are led by the Holy Spirit to the end of Revelation, we'll see that this deceiver will be captured and thrown into the bottomless pit for a thousand years during the Lord's Millennial reign, then he will be released and draw people away by sin in staggering numbers (Revelation:20-8). He will go out to deceive the nations called Gog and Magog in every corner of the earth. He will gather them together for battle, a mighty army as numberless as sand along the seashore.

Remember, they have been living with God the Father and the Lord Jesus for this thousand-year reign. In my last book, Two Steps from the End, I used a time machine to travel around the scriptures. Let's knock off the dust and the rust, fire it up and head through these stories to look at the depravity of the mind of man. Let's get into this old-time machine, grab our compass and map and head to Genesis 6:7, The Days of Noah, where the Lord said he was sorry that He made them (man and woman). He is compassionate, holy, gracious, righteous, merciful, forgiving, and wrathful. He is God. Isaiah 55:8(NKJ) says, for My thoughts are not your thoughts nor are your ways my ways, says the Lord. For as the heavens are higher than the earth, so my ways are higher than your ways and my thoughts than your thoughts. In Verse 11, it was the same with my Word.

I send it out and it always produces fruit. It will accomplish all I want it to and it will prosper everywhere I send it (Isaiah 40:21-24). (Living Bible)

Haven't you heard? Don't you understand? Are you deaf to the words of God, the words He gave before the world began? Are you so ignorant (Verse 22). God sits above the circle of the earth. The people below seem like grasshoppers to him (He knows when we sit down and when we will stand). He knows our thoughts before the thoughts enter our minds. He holds our very breath. He spreads out the heavens like a curtain and makes his tent from them. He judges the great people of the world and brings them all to nothing. They hardly get started, barely taking root, when he blows on them and they wither. The wind carries them off like chaff (Verse 26). Look up into the heavens, who created all the stars? He brings them out like an army, one after another calling, each by its name with his great power and incomparable strength – not a single one is missing.

We can only see the events of the world through the news – if we can believe the news. But God sees everything, everywhere, every second of the day. We see the love of God the Father when He gave His son for our sins. We see what Jesus did for us on the cross (John 10:18).(Living Bible) No one can take my life from me, I sacrifice it voluntarily, for I have the authority to lay it down when I want and also to take it up again, for this is what my Heavenly Father has commanded (2 Peter 3:9).(Living Bible)

The Lord isn't really being as slow about his promise that some people think. No, he is being patient for your sake. He doesn't want anyone to be destroyed but wants everyone to repent (to be born again). Then the heavens will pass away with a terrible noise. The very elements themselves will disappear in fire and earth, and everything on it will be found to deserve judgment. As sure as God's love cannot be measured, we can know that God's judgment on the sins of this world is coming (Verse 15). Remember that our Lord's patience gives everyone time to be saved (Verse 17). You already know these things dear friends so be on guard, so that you will not be carried away by the errors of wicked people and lose your own secure footing. Rather, you must grow in the grace and knowledge of our Lord and Savior Jesus Christ.

Now we have to dig into the days of Noah. I'm going to use Jeff Kinley's book - his in-depth study of the days Noah was on the earth. I'll use Jeff's words in this powerful book, a riveting read and a stunning preview of Earth's final days. There are warnings from Bible prophecy, Genesis 6:5 that says "The Lord saw that the wickedness of man was great, and that every intent of the thoughts of his heart was evil continually." In fact, throughout the Bible, God repeatedly declares that the human heart is full of sin, even going so far as to say that it is deceitful above all things and desperately wicked. This is total depravity. In Matthew 12:34(NKJ) Jesus said, "brood of vipers! How can you being evil speak good things? For out of the abundance of the heart the mouth speaks. A good man out of the good treasures of his heart, brings forth good things, and an evil man out of the evil treasure brings forth evil things. But I say to you that for every idle word man may speak, they will give account of it in the Day of Judgement. For by your words, you will be justified, and by your words you will be condemned."

Let's head back to Genesis, in that old-time machine, and continue in The archives of Noah and the decline of the human race. Lord at the end of the road, when I get to the final destination at the foot of your cross, let me be able to stand before you and say, like Paul, I finished the race you set before me.

I don't know what the future holds, but Father, I know that the future is in your hands. Long before God's Judgment came upon these people, they were already busy defiling the earth with their sin and evil. They actually were as bad as they could be all the time. "Then the Lord saw that the wickedness of man was great on the earth and that every intent of their thoughts of the heart was only evil continually." certainly, those evil thoughts would have included sexual promiscuity, adultery, perversion, as well as rape, prostitution, homosexuality and lesbianism. It is not a stretch to imagine how prominent they would have been in a world without any moral compass or restraint.

The Lord says that as the end draws near evil will wax worse and worse. What would sex and sexuality look like if mankind's worst and most vile imaginings were permitted, even encouraged. You can imagine that when the Antichrist and false prophet come on the scene Satan is leading the way, just as he was behind the perversion of Noah's day and the days of Lot. In the perversion of today he is also out front, leading the way. The Nephilim were on the earth in those days and also afterwards, when the sons of God came to the daughters of men, and those daughters bore children for them. Those were the mighty men - the old men of renown. What does this mean, Sons of God Nephilim? When Satan was kicked out of Heaven, one-third of the angels were kicked out too, so what is being stated here is that demonic entities had sex with these women on earth. These were super beings, and we can see how corrupt this society had become when we see what the Lord saw, that the wickedness of man was so great on the earth, and that every intent of the thoughts of his heart was only evil continually. Now the earth was corrupt in the sight of God and the earth was filled with violence, and no home was safe, perhaps even from its own family members. It's not difficult to imagine widespread domestic violence and such a savage society. In Mark 13:12 (Living Bible)It says "A brother will betray his brother to the death, a father will betray his own child, and children will rebel against their parents and cause them to be killed. And everyone will hate you because you are my followers. But the one who endures to the end will be saved." Jesus told us that this will happen in the end. Women were not innocent. They were enslaved by evil and also violent.

Noah found favor in the eyes of the Lord because Noah was a man who walked with God (Genesis 6:8). God spoke to Noah and charged him with this bizarre command. He gave him the blueprint for building a massive ship. This ship was 450 feet long, 75 feet wide, 45 feet high, and a hundred feet longer than a football field - including the end zones. It was constructed out of gopher wood. Once cut, hewn, and planed, the wood would then be sealed with pitch, a glue-like substance made from resin. This was such an undertaking! Imagine cutting down the tree, removing the bark, then hewing and planing every log to fit with precise accuracy. Imagine this man's daily grind - day in and day out. I'm sure he was the laughing stock. Just like other men and women of scripture, they fought the fight that God gave them. David facing the giant, Moses leading over a million people out of exile into the unknown, Gideon being called to save Israel, the disciples, Paul called to write over half of the New Testament, and all of the others.

Noah had a battle-hardened faith. How strong would your faith be if everyone was against you and thought you were a fool? God asked him to do this, and to include even the smallest details. God tests our faith, and we have to be willing to saw, sweat, hammer and hurt. Sometimes God calls you out onto the battlefield to face the giants of our lives, like David.

Then God commanded the shipbuilder and his entire family to enter the Ark. They ascended the long ramp and entered the ship for safety. Following them was a parade of paired animals brought to Noah by God "for a full seven days before the rain fell". The time had passed for preaching one last sermon in hopes that someone, or anyone, would respond to his message of repentance and salvation, but those words fell on deaf ears, and calloused and hardened hearts.

God's grace, compassion and patience ran out. God closed the door behind them with a thud that could probably be heard for miles. Echoing the floodgates of Heaven, the sky opened and rain fell upon the earth for forty days and forty nights. God's tolerance for man's rebellion had come to an end. He blotted out every living thing. Jesus confirmed this event as well as the days of Lot which we are going to cover.

Bible prophecies alert us regarding the end times. They warn of approaching danger regarding the end times. We have seen some of the similarities between Noah's day and the final days on planet Earth. We cannot become complacent, but must heed the warning Jesus has given us. Saying we have heard this for years must not harden our hearts to the warnings. If we listen hard enough, we can hear the approaching hoofbeats of the Apocalypse.

Chapter 7

Guess Who's Coming to Dinner:

Let us fire up that time machine and set the date for Genesis 18. We have an appearance of Jesus in the Old Testament. Jesus and two angels came through the camp of Abraham to tell him and his wife, Sarah, that the promise that God gave to them twenty-five years earlier of having a son would come to pass, although Sarah, at age 90, was past child-bearing years, and Abraham was 100 years old. But there is another part to this story. The second part occurs when Jesus and the two angels were on their way to destroy Sodom and Gomorrah. Let's listen to this conversation between Jesus and Abraham. (God's Judgment is Coming: Genesis 18:22).(Living Bible))

The other men (angels) turned and headed toward Sodom, but the Lord remained with Abraham. Abraham approached him and asked, "Will you sweep away both the righteous and the wicked? Suppose you find fifty righteous people living there in the city. Will you sweep it away and not spare it for their sakes? Surely you would not do such a thing, destroying the righteous along with the wicked. Why, you would be treating the righteous and the wicked exactly the same! Surely you would not do that! Should not the Judge of all the earth do what is right? At this point I am going back to verses

16-21.(Living Bible) There are some riches in God's Word that I missed. Then the men (angels) got up from their meal and looked toward Sodom. Even though this scripture verse was not written in Hebrews 13:2,(Living Bible) Don't forget to show hospitality to strangers, for some who have done this have entertained angels without realizing it. As they left, Abraham went with them to send them on their way. Should I hide my plan from Abraham? the Lord asked. For Abraham will certainly become a great and mighty nation, and all the nations of the earth will be blessed through him.

I have singled him out so that he will direct his sons and their families to keep the ways of the Lord by doing what is right and just. Then I will do for Abraham all that I have promised. Read this again: Jesus is speaking as God in the flesh, telling Abraham about his life - just as he knows our lives.

So, the Lord told Abraham, I have heard a great cry from Sodom and Gomorrah because their sin is so flagrant (something considered wrong or immoral; conspicuously or obviously offensive). I am going down to see if they are as wicked as I have heard. If not, I want to know.

And the Lord replied, "If I find fifty righteous people in Sodom, I will spare the entire city for their sake."

Then Abraham spoke again: Since I have begun, let me speak further to my Lord, even though I am just dust and ashes. Suppose there are only forty-five righteous people rather than fifty? Will you destroy the whole for the lack of five?

And the Lord said, "I will not destroy it if I find forty-five righteous people there."

Then Abraham pressed his request further. "Suppose there are only forty?" And the Lord replied, "I will not destroy it for the sake of forty."

"Please don't be angry, my Lord", Abraham pleaded. "Let me speak - suppose there are only thirty righteous?" And the Lord replied, "I will not destroy it if I find thirty." Then Abraham said, "Since I have dared to speak to the Lord let me continue - suppose there are only twenty?" And the Lord replied, "Then I will not destroy it for the sake of the twenty."

Finally, Abraham said, "Lord please don't be angry with me if I speak one more time. Suppose only ten are found there?"

And the Lord replied, "Then I will not destroy it for the sake of the ten." When the Lord had finished his conversation with Abraham he went on his way, and Abraham returned to his tent.

Chapter 8

Run for Your Life:

That evening, the two angels came to the entrance of the city of Sodom. Lot was sitting, and when he stood up to meet them, he welcomed them and bowed his face to the ground. "My lords", he said, "come to my home to wash your feet, and be my guests for the night. You may then get up early in the morning and be on your way" (remember that out of this cesspool of sin came sodomy). "Oh, no", they replied. "We'll just spend the night out here in the city square."

But Lot insisted, so at last they went home with him. Lot prepared a feast for them, complete with fresh bread made without yeast, and they ate. Before they retired for the night, all the men of Sodom, young and old, came from all over the city and surrounded the house. They shouted to Lot to bring out the men who came to spend the night - to bring them out so that they could have sex with them. Lot stepped outside to talk to them, shutting the door behind him. He begged them not to do such a wicked thing (Lot realized it was wicked). He told them that he had two virgin daughters and that he would bring them out to them, and that they could do with them whatever they wished. Wait! Wait - did I read that right? Lot was offering his daughters to these perverts. He pleaded with them to leave the men alone because they were his guests and are under his protection.

At this point, I want to fire up the time machine and head to Babylon, Daniel 5, and Belshazzar, predecessor of Nebuchadnezzar (this is a knee knocking moment for Belshazzer)Let's look at how Belshazzar pushed God's love, mercy and patience to the limit.

Many years later, King Belshazzar gave a great feast for 1,000 of his nobles, and he drank wine with them. While Belshazzar was drinking wine, he gave orders to bring in the gold and silver cups that his predecessor, Nebuchadnezzar, had taken from the Temple in Jerusalem. He wanted to drink from them with his nobles, his wives and his concubines. So, they drank from the gold and silver cups, and while they drank from them, they praised their idols made of gold, silver, bronze, iron, wood and stone.

Suddenly, they saw the fingers of a human hand writing on the plaster wall of the King's palace near the lampstand. The King himself saw the hand as it wrote, 'The handwriting is on the wall' (this is where the old adage comes from), and his face turned pale with fright. His knees knocked together in fear and his legs gave way beneath him.

The King shouted for the enchanters, astrologers and fortune-tellers (occultic practices) to be brought before him. He told these wise men of Babylon that whoever could read the writing and tell him what it meant would be dressed in purple robes of royal honor and would have gold chains placed around his neck, and that he would become the third highest ruler in the kingdom!

But when all the king's wise men had come in, none could read the writing or tell the King what it meant. So, the King grew even more alarmed and his face again turned pale. His nobles, too, were shaken.

But when the Queen Mother heard what was happening, she hurried to the banquet hall. She said to Belshazzar, "Long live the King! Don't be so frightened. There is a man in your kingdom who has within him the spirit of the holy gods. During Nebuchadnezzar's reign, this man was found to have insight, understanding and wisdom like that of gods. Your predecessor the King Nebuchadnezzar made him chief over all the magicians, enchanters, astrologers and fortune-tellers of Babylon. This man Daniel, as the king named him. Belshazzar has exceptional ability and is filled with divine knowledge and understanding. He can interpret dreams, explain riddles and solve difficult problems. Call for Daniel and he will tell you what the writing means.

So, Daniel was brought before the King. The King asked him, "Are you Daniel, one of the exiles brought to Judah by my predecessor, King Nebuchadnezzar?

I have heard that you have the spirit of the gods within you, and that you are filled with insight, understanding and wisdom. My wise men and enchanters have tried to read the words on the wall and tell me their meaning, but they cannot do it. I am told that you can give interpretations and solve difficult problems. If you can read these words and tell me their meaning, you will be clothed in purple robes of royal honor, and you will have a gold chain placed around your neck. You will become the third highest ruler of the kingdom."

Daniel answered the King, "Keep your gifts or give them to someone else, but I will tell you what the writing means, Your Majesty, the Most-High God gave sovereignty, majesty, glory and honor to your predecessor, Nebuchadnezzar. He made him so great that people of all races and nations and languages trembled before him in fear. He killed those he wanted to kill and spared those he wanted to spare. He honored those he wanted to honor and disgraced those he wanted to disgrace. But when his head and mind were puffed with arrogance, he was brought down from his royal throne and stripped of his glory. He was driven from human society. He was given the mind of a wild animal and he lived among the wild donkeys. He ate grass like a cow and he was drenched with the dew of heaven until he learned that the Most-High God rules over the kingdom of the world and appoints anyone he desires to rule.

You are his successor, Belshazzar, and you knew this, yet you have not humbled yourself, for you have proudly defied the Lord of Heaven and have had these cups from his temple brought before you. You and your nobles and your wives and concubines have been drinking wine from them while praising gods of silver, gold, bronze, iron, wood and stone - gods that neither see nor hear nor know anything at all. But you have not honored the God who gives you the breath of life and holds your destiny! So, God has sent this hand to write this message. This is the message that was written: Mene, Mene Tekel and Parson. This is what these words mean: Mene means numbered - God has numbered the days of your reign and has brought it to an end. Tekel means weighed - you have been weighed on the balances and have not measured up. Parsin means divided - your kingdom has been divided to the Meades and Persians.

Then, at Belshazzar's command, Daniel was dressed in purple, a gold chain was hung around his neck and he was proclaimed the third highest ruler in the kingdom.

That very night, Belshazzar the Babylonian king was killed, and Darius the Meade took over the kingdom at the age of sixty-two.

From this point we're going to fire up that old time-machine and set the date back to Genesis 18. God's judgment is about to fall upon Sodom and Gomorrah. *Stand back!* they shouted. *This fellow came to town as an outsider, and now he is acting like our Judge! We'll treat you far worse than those other men!* And they lunged toward Lot to break down the door.

But the two angels reached out, pulled Lot into the house and bolted the door. Then they blinded all the men, young and old, who were at the door of the house, so they gave up trying to get inside.

Meanwhile, the angels questioned Lot. *Do you have any other relatives here in the city?* they asked. "Get them out of this place - your sons-in-law, sons, daughters or anyone else. For we are about to destroy this city completely." Just as in Noah's day, Judgment will be swift and happen quickly. "The outcry against this place is so great that it has reached the Lord and he has sent us to destroy it."

So, Lot rushed out to tell his daughters' fiancés, quick, get out of the city! The Lord is about to destroy it! But the young men thought he was only joking.

At dawn the next morning, the angels became insistent. "Hurry!" they said to Lot. "Take your wife and your two daughters who are here. Get out right now, or you will be swept away in the destruction of the city!"

When Lot continued to hesitate, the angels seized his hand and the hands of his wife and two daughters, and rushed them to safety outside of the city, for the Lord was merciful. When they were safely out of the city, one of the angels ordered, "Run for your lives, and don't look back or stop anywhere in the valley! Escape to the mountains or you will be swept away!"

"Oh no, my Lord!" Lot begged. "You have been so gracious to me and saved my life, and you have shown me such great kindness. But I cannot go to the mountains. Disaster would catch up to me there, and I would soon die. See, there is a small village nearby, please let me go there instead. Don't you see how small it is? Then my life will be saved."

"Alright," the angel said. "I will grant your request. I will not destroy the little village. But hurry! escape to it, for I can do nothing until you arrive there." This explains why that village was known as Zoar, which means 'little place').

Lot reached the village just as the sun was rising over the horizon. Then the Lord rained down fire and burning sulfur from the sky on Sodom and Gomorrah. He utterly destroyed them, along with the other cities and villages of the plain, wiping out all the people and every bit of vegetation. But Lot's wife looked back as she was following behind him, and she turned into a pillar of salt. She disobeyed God. The angels had told her not to look back, but she was still drawn to her old life (I ICorinthians 5:17). This means that anyone who belongs to Christ has become a new person. The old life is gone, and a new life has begun. Let's now fly over to Romans I, dig into the archives of Paul's writing, and dig deep for the hidden riches of God's Word.

Romans I:18.Living Bible) But God shows his anger from Heaven against all sinful, wicked people who suppress the truth by their wickedness. They know the truth about God because he has made it obvious to them. For, ever since the world was created, people have seen the earth and sky. Through everything God made they can clearly see his invisible qualities - his eternal power and divine nature. They have no excuse for not knowing God.

Yes, they knew God, but they would not worship him as God, or even give him thanks, and they began to think up foolish ideas of what God was like. As a result, their minds became dark and confused. Claiming to be wise, they instead became utter fools, and instead of worshiping the glorious ever-living God, they worshiped idols made to look like mere people and birds and animals and reptiles.

So, God abandoned them to do whatever shameful things their hearts desired, and as a result, they did vile and degrading things with other bodies. They traded the truth about God for a lie, so they worshiped and served the things God had created instead of the Creator himself, who is worthy of eternal praise! Amen.

That is why God abandoned them to their shameful desires. Even the women turned against the natural way to have sex, and instead indulged in sex with each other. The men, instead of having normal sexual relations with women, burned with lust for each other. Men did shameful things with other men, and as a result of this sin they suffered within themselves the penalty that they deserved.

Since they thought it foolish to acknowledge God, he abandoned them to their foolish thinking and let them do things that should never be done. Their lives became full of every kind of wickedness and sin: greed, hate, envy, murder, quarreling, deception, malicious behavior and gossip. They are back-stabbers and haters of God - insolent, proud and boastful. They invent new ways of sinning and they disobey their parents. They refuse to understand, break their promises, are heartless and have no mercy. They know that God's justice requires that those who do these things deserve to die, yet they do them anyway. Worse yet, they encourage others to do them as well.

What do we say Lord God, wake up America, and not only America, but the entire world? As we see in these three stories, Satan has taken down these societies to the depravity of their minds and lifestyle (II Timothy 3:1).(NKJ) But know this - that in the last days perilous times will come.

If we listen, we can hear the four horsemen of the apocalypse fast approaching. God's Judgements are coming. Matthew 24:21(NKJ) says, for then there will be great tribulation such as has not been since the beginning of the world until this time, nor ever shall be. Heaven and earth will pass away but my Word will never pass away.

At this point, I'm going to get into the stealth rider, head across the Arabian Desert to Babylon and dig into the archives of Daniel. But first, we are going to stop economic collapse in the last days prior to the Great Tribulation, and the return of our great God and Savior Jesus Christ. I'm going to unlock the treasures of Dr. David Jeremiah's book, 'The Coming of Economic Armageddon', and what Bible prophecy warns about the New Global Economy.

I've been blessed by his teachings for years. He has written several God inspired books. He has a radio program called Turning Point. He pastors Shadow Mountain Community Church in El Cajon, California. If you want to be blessed, look him up on the radio or television and he will take you on an in-depth study into the riches of God's Holy Word. He also takes God's Word across these United States to look for his crusade in a big city near you.

When David wrote this book, I believe in 2008 or 2009 (I don't know when but it doesn't matter), the national debt at that time was 12 trillion dollars. Today (2020) it is $24 trillion dollars and growing, especially as the pandemic hit in 2020. This one virus has turned the economy of the world upside down. Just the interest on this $24 trillion national debt is what the federal government must pay on the outstanding public debt each year. The interest on the debt is $479 billion. That is from the federal budget for fiscal year 2020, that runs from October 1, 2019 through September 30, 2020.

David gave this analogy regarding billions and trillions of dollars, and it is staggering. The Federal Reserve issues new hundred-dollar bills to banks in small packs of $100 bills each, or 10,000 per pack. One hundred of these packs equals $1,000,000. Ten thousand of these packs equals $100,000,000 - the amount that can sit on a standard industrial pallet in a neat cube of bills. Ten of those pallets could fit into the average living room, holding $1,000,000,000,000. or $1 trillion (hold on - this is mind blowing). You could spend $1 million a day, every day, since the birth of Christ, and still not spend a trillion dollars.

Today, in April, 2020, I sit here - due to the fact that the pandemic has tanked the U.S. economy. Within a few weeks our economy was rolling, but we've gone into a nose-dive.

I'm sure you've heard the term 'New World Order' - a one world government. Especially because we sit here today in shut-down status, people are asking if the virus can be transmitted through the exchange of money. Our credit cards now come with a chip in them and with our information on that chip. You insert your card and it is read within seconds. When the Antichrist comes on the scene, you will not be able to buy or sell without using his mark.

Jesus referred to the events leading up to his return as birth pangs. Starting out, the pain is not as intense as just before the birth of the child. It will be the same with the coming Kingdom of God: pain and discomfort on a global scale. The world began experiencing discomfort in a serious way with the 2008 economic birth pangs - unprecedented degrees of pain and suffering around the world.

As I sit here today, the world's economy is in turmoil. Unemployment is closing in on numbers equal to the Great Depression. They are trying to jumpstart the economy, opening up states that weren't hit so hard, not knowing what the results will be, and trying to get people back to work with social distancing. Students of biblical prophecy will not be caught off guard by these developments. As far back as the prophet Daniel foretold, there will arise an end time when government will be led by the most ruthless dictator in history. This leader will be Satan's CEO, empowered by the devil. People who are hungry will swear allegiance to him rather than starve.

The Coming Economic Armageddon has been written to help you understand what was foretold in the past, what is happening right now, and how to prepare for the future. Most of all, it has been prepared to encourage you to put your trust and hope in God – the One who knows the beginning from the end, the One who is surprised by nothing, the One who can deliver you safely through the economic storms of our day. The 'bail-out' money system makes each existing dollar worth less than before. It then takes more dollars to purchase the item today than it did yesterday, and this is called inflation.

The Bible says that life on planet earth will become very dark and difficult prior to the return of Christ, so we should not be surprised at what we see happening in our world. These days should motivate us to take the Gospel and our understanding of Biblical Prophecy into a world living in confusion and despair. We have the only message that will survive the present and future upheavals the world may witness. May God grant us the courage to speak and live with biblical clarity in the days ahead.

End Time Prophecies Seen Through the Eyes of Daniel:

Let us fire up the stealth rider, put our pedal down, and move across the terrain of the Arabian Desert to Babylon, where we will dig into the archives of Daniel, this man of God. His name means 'God is my Judge'. God is all of our Judge (Hebrews 9:27),(Living Bible) And just as each person is destined to die once and, thereafter, comes Judgment.

As a young teenager, Daniel and several friends were taken to Babylon in the first group of captives. There Daniel was trained with young men from other districts of the empire of Babylon. Through a series of events recorded in his book, Daniel was advanced to the highest positions in the administration of three empires, and his life spans the entire period of Judah's captivity. God's hand was on his servant Daniel. Daniel never wavered in his loyalty to his God. He did not succumb to these pagan empires and their false gods. We'll look at the shape of history ahead as the Bible describes it in one of the most fascinating of Bible prophetic books.

What I want to dig into a story in Daniel and an appearance of Jesus in the Old Testament. These three young men went with Daniel when they were taken captive from Israel to Babylon. Let's unlock the treasure of this story. Let's call it 'A Walk with God'. Let's see how Shadrach, Meshach and Abed-Nego defied the King and made a stand for God.

At that time Chaldeans came forward and accused the Jews. They spoke and said to King Nebuchadnezzar, "O King, live forever! You, O King live forever, have made a decree that everyone who hears the sound of the horn, flute, harp, lyre and psalter in symphony with all kinds of music, shall fall down and worship the gold image, and whoever does not fall down and worship the gold image shall be cast into the midst of a burning, fiery furnace.

There are certain Jews whom you have set over the affairs of the Province of Babylon. Shadrach, Meshach and Abed-Nego, these men O King, have not paid homage to you. They do not serve your gods or worship the gold image which you set up."

Then Nebuchadnezzar, enraged and furious, commanded them to bring Shadrach, Meshach and Abed-Nego. They brought these men before him. King Nebuchadnezzar spoke to them saying, "Is it true, Shadrach, Meshach and Abed-Nego, that you do not serve my gods or worship the gold image which I have set up? Now, if you are ready at the time when you hear the sound of the horn, flute, harp, lyre and psalter in symphony with all kinds of music, and you fall down and worship the image which I have made – good! But if you do not worship, you shall be cast immediately into the midst of a burning, fiery furnace. And who is the God who will deliver you from my hands?" Nebuchadnezzar had an *I* problem – he was full of himself. With a series of events, God humbled this man so much that he lost his mind. He ate grass from the field like a wild animal. Shadrach, Meshach and Abed-Nego answered and said to the King, "O Nebuchadnezzar, we have no need to answer you in this matter. If that is the case, our God whom we serve is able to deliver us from the burning, fiery furnace, and He will deliver us from your hand O King. But, if not, let it be known to you, O King, that we do not serve your gods, nor will we worship the gold image which you have set up."

Then Nebuchadnezzar was full of fury and the expression on his face changed toward Shadrach, Meshach and Abed-Nego. He spoke and commanded that they heat the furnace seven times hotter than it was usually heated. He commanded certain mighty men of valor who were in his army to bind Shadrach, Meshach and Abed-Nego, and cast them into the burning, fiery furnace. These men were then bound in their coats, their trousers, their turbans and other garments, and were cast into the midst of the fiery furnace.

The king's command was urgent and the furnace exceedingly hot. The flames of the fire killed those men who took up Shadrach, Meshach and Abed-Nego and cast them into the fire, and these three men, Shadrach, Meshach and Abed-Nego, fell down, bound into the midst of the fiery furnace.

King Nebuchadnezzar was astonished, and he rose in haste and said to his counselors, "Did we not cast three bound men into the midst of the fire?"

They turned and said to the king, "True, O king."

"Look!", he exclaimed, "I see four men loose, walking in the midst of the fire, and they are not hurt, and the form of the fourth is like the Son of God." "I will never fail you I will never abandon you." (Hebrews 13:5)(Living Bible)

No matter what we are facing in life, He is always a prayer away. He is by our side. He will walk through the fire with you. As we see with Moses, He will hold back the waters. He will stretch out his arms and be nailed to a cross for us.

Nebuchadnezzar then went near the mouth of the burning, fiery furnace and spoke, saying Shadrach, Meshach and Abed-Nego, servants of the Most-High God, come out and come here. And they came out unscathed and committed.

David is portrayed as a distinct and humble man, although he rose to the highest governmental rank and was familiar with several world rulers. Here is a legacy every man should strive for. It is said that Daniel was portrayed as a humble man, and that he maintained his daily walk with God. Ezekiel set Daniel as a standard for his wisdom, and this is so true. God used him to interpret Nebuchadnezzar's dreams and the handwriting on the wall with Belshazzar's. Also, the Lord gave him a prophetic view of the future. The Book of Daniel has been scrutinized more than any other of the prophetic books of the Old Testament. Jesus himself authenticates his prophecies in Matthew 24:15 and in Mark 13:14, and we see Nebuchadnezzar honoring the Most-High God:

> For His dominion is an eternal dominion; And His kingdom is from generation to generation. All the inhabitants of the earth are reputed as nothing. He does according to his will with the army of Heaven and the peoples of the earth. No one can restrain His hand or say to Him, "What have you done?"
>
> Daniel 4:34-35(NKJ)

God chose to stand behind the scenes of history for the most part. But when He chooses, He can and will intervene. Even behind the scenes, He is the author and director of the play. So, history and the future move purposefully toward what He has planned.

Someday the Messiah will come. Someday the kingdoms of the world will be shaken. Someday all worldly glory will be shattered. There is someone like the Son of Man, Jesus (Daniel 7:13). To Him, the Ancient of Days, Jesus would make a great presentation. We're looking ahead to a great presentation. Looking ahead in a great vision of the night, Daniel's destiny.

He was given authority, glory and sovereign power over all peoples and nations, and men of every language worshiped him. His dominion is an everlasting dominion that will not pass away, and his Kingdom is one that will never be destroyed (Daniel 7:14). In Isaiah 42:9,(NKJ) Behold the former things have come to pass.And new things I declare Before they spring forth.

The Book of Daniel contains some of the most spectacular prophecies. Many of Daniel's prophecies are yet to be fulfilled. Some of the prophetic themes laced throughout this book concern world empires from Babylon to the times of Christ, the Coming of the Messiah, and the days of the Antichrist.

Do not learn to imitate the detestable ways of the nations. Let no one be found among you who sacrifices his son or daughter on the fire, who practices divination or sorcery, interprets omens, or engages in witchcraft, or casts spells, or who is a medium or practices spiritism, or who consults the dead. Anyone who does these things is detestable to the Lord (Deuteronomy 18:9-12).

God committed Himself to speak to the Old Testament believers through the prophets. In those days, as in ours, believers are to walk by faith in obedience to the written Word. This is the decisive test. What the prophet predicts must always come true!

Daniel records not only the miraculous interpretation of Nebuchadnezzar's first dream, but also the prophecy of Nebuchadnezzar's madness.

The events in Daniel are not in chronological order. The visions in chapters seven and eight occur between the events of chapters four and five, and the discussion with the archangel in chapter nine occurred between chapters five and six. A perspective is coming directly from Jesus. Then we will look at the events leading up to Gabriel's words about the seventy weeks. God did this in order to deliver this amazing prophecy.

Matthew's accounts offer more information because Matthew was a tax collector. News in shorthand was prevalent in those days.

As Jesus was there upon the Mount of Olives, these four disciples came to him privately saying, "Tell us when shall be the sign of thy coming and the end of the world?" (Math. 24:3).(Living Bible)

They asked him three questions and Jesus answered them. Jesus answered and said unto them, "Take heed that no man may deceive you." He opens and closes this time together, warning them not to be deceived. How do we do this? We have the Truth of God's Word comparing scripture to scripture. Let the Holy Spirit lead us in the Truth of God's Word.

Jesus tells them not to be deceived, then he says do not be troubled. These things must come to pass, but the end is not yet.

Nation will rise against nation, kingdom against kingdom. There will be famine and pestilence and earthquakes in diverse places. All these things are the beginning of sorrows. People believe he is saying this prior to his coming, but Jesus said these things will happen. Jesus is talking to his Jewish disciples. He is not talking to the Gentile believers. Then Jesus said in Matthew 24:5, this is prophecy from Daniel, when ye therefore shall see the abomination of desolation (after the Jewish temple is built the Antichrist will enter and claim that he is God) spoken of by Daniel the prophet, stand in the Holy place (whoso readeth let him understand). Then let them which are in Judea flee into the mountains. As Jesus said *whoso readeth let him understand*. This message is for everyone. God intends for each person to understand it.

There are claims that Daniel was written by multiple writers, but Jesus identifies Daniel as a prophet and He does something even more. He points to this very passage in Daniel 9, referring to this abomination of desolation.

This is when the statue of the Antichrist is placed in the temple, both as the Antichrist enters the temple and claims to be God. Then it says they will make this statue of the Antichrist's image speak. With computer technology this could happen today. When John wrote this, he did not know what he was seeing. Idols were always considered to be an abomination. So, when the Antichrist and false prophet put this pagan idol in the Holy of Holies, *Look out!* The world will see this on cable tv worldwide. Jesus said, unless those days be shortened, no one on this earth will survive. In Daniel 7,(NKJ) We have the Picture of the Ancient of Days seated in Judgment, destroying the final enemy. Then with clouds of Heaven, a Son of Man comes to receive dominion and glory and the Kingdom. He rules forever.

In Daniel 8, we again see the final enemy destroyed by the Prince of Princes, but only after the very sanctuary of God has suffered revolting sacrilege (v. 13). The later prophecy is not explained to Daniel, for his angelic interpreter reports that the vision concerns the time of the end (v.17).

Jesus said in Matthew 24:16-17,(Living Bible) Then let them which be in Juda flee into the mountains. Let him which is on the housetop not come down to take anything out of his house.

Houses in Israel were built on the hillside because it is a hilly terrain. The roof is their patio. They have to go downstairs to get back into the house. When Jesus is telling them not to come down, He's saying run - get out of there.

Neither let him which is in the field return back to take his clothes. And woe unto them that are with child and to them that give suck in those days! But pray ye that your flight be not in the winter, neither on the Sabbath Day (Matthew 24:18-20)(NKJ). Jesus warns about returning to grab supplies, even essentials such as clothing. Flee for your life.

The last comments refer to the Sabbath. Focus is on Israel and the Jews and directing this to his disciples, who are Jewish. Matthew 24:21(NKJ) Says, for then shall be great tribulation such as was not since the beginning of the world to this time nor ever shall be.

He is quoting from Daniel 12. Jesus Himself labels the last half of the seven years as the great tribulation. When Jesus said unless the days be shortened, there would be no flesh saved, this could only happen in the days we live in, or the future. It could happen with the nuclear weapons we have today, as they keep advancing. For example, during the Civil War this could not have happened. World War I - no. In World War II, we discovered the hydrogen bomb and nuclear power. Now third world countries like India and Pakistan have nuclear weapons.

This is known as the interrupted prayer. For the first nineteen verses, Daniel is praying. Then the angel Gabriel appears and interrupts his prayer. Gabriel then gives Daniel the most intriguing verse in God's Word (Daniel 7. 24-27).

Daniel was reading his Bible, the Book of Jeremiah. Jeremiah talks about the seventy years of captivity. Daniel is very precise - he knows the seventy years are about over. He knew seventy years was prophesied in Jeremiah 25:11. And it shall come to pass, when seventy years are accomplished, that I will punish the King of Babylon. For thus sayeth the Lord, that after seventy years be accomplished at Babylon, I will visit you and perform my good word toward you, in causing you to return to this place (Jeremiah 29:10).(NKJ)

This was written in Jerusalem and twice in the Book of Jeremiah. Daniel could cling to this promise. Daniel 9:3(NKJ) says, Then I set my face unto the Lord God to make request by prayer and supplications, with fasting and sackcloth and ashes.

The prophecy of the 70 weeks began when the decree went forth to rebuild the city of Jerusalem. The angel Gabriel told Daniel that 483 years after that decree, Messiah, the Prince, would come forth. Exactly 483 years later, Jesus entered the city of Jerusalem and presented Himself as Messiah to His people.

God's program for Israel according to Daniel will encompass a total of 69 weeks (which are years) that will begin on a particular day and end on a particular day. There will be a gap in time, and finally there will be the seventieth week. We understand that the 69 weeks in Daniel refer to groups of years and that a week refers to a group of seven years, so the total is 483 years (69x7).

There will be a separation in Daniel's prophecy after the sixty-ninth week, a great gap - the great parenthesis. Where does that gap come from? In 9:24 we discover that the 70 weeks, or 490 years, are determined in order. Six things will happen:

1. To finish the transgression.
2. To make amend of sins.
3. To make reconciliation for iniquity.
4. To bring in everlasting righteousness.
5. To seal up vision and prophesy.
6. To anoint the Most Holy.

Not one of these prophecies was fulfilled in the 69 weeks. So, there must be a future time for God's people. In that time the final seven-year tribulation period will begin.

The seventieth week in Daniel's prophecy: Once the church is raptured out of the world, in the final seven-year period of Daniel, tribulation begins: "He (the Prince) shall confirm a covenant with many for one week, but in the middle of the week he shall bring an end to sacrifice and offering. And on the wing of abominations shall be one who makes desolate, even until the consummation which is determined is poured out on the desolate." (9:27).(NKJ)

Daniel mentions two princes: Messiah, the Prince (9:25),(NKJ) who is Jesus Christ and "the prince who is to come, the Antichrist (9:26-27).NKJ) The seventieth week is interrupted. The text says "in the middle of the week". Halfway through the first, or three and a half years after making peace in Israel, the Antichrist will break the treaty and do away with the Jewish sacrifices. The result will be the Great Tribulation - the last three and a half years when God's Judgment will be felt around the world.

The time of the Great Tribulation is called the time of Jacob, Trouble is described in Matthew 24:15-21(Living Bible) by the Lord Jesus. "Therefore, when you see the abomination of desolation spoken of by Daniel the Prophet, standing in the Holy Place, then there will be great tribulation such as has not been since the beginning of the world until this time, no nor ever shall be. It's coming. It may be on the horizon, but it's coming. Jesus said it, and we have to believe it. Then Jesus will reign everlasting righteousness during the millennium. He will be King of Kings.

Daniel Chapter 12:11. And at that time shall Michael stand up, the great prince which standeth for the children of thy people: and there shall be a time of trouble such as never was since there was a nation (even) to that same time; and at that time thy people shall be delivered, every one that shall be found written in the book.

In Chapter 11 of Daniel we were brought to the time of the end. Notice the word 'and' which connects this with the end of the last chapter, which was speaking of the last chapter, which was speaking of the willful king, the Antichrist.

During the Great Tribulation there will be an unprecedented attack to exterminate the Jews, but will be delivered by Michael the archangel.

First of all, we must see that Michael is a ministering spirit to the believers. He is actually an archangel over the other angels. His ministry is directly under the instruction of the Lord Jesus Christ.

We know the time mentioned here is the end of the Gentile age. This points back to 11:36-45, the time of the ascendance of the Antichrist during the final tribulation period. During that period of Michael, the archangel (Jude 9-10)Yet Michael the archangel, there are ministers paying special attention to protecting Israel during that Gentile time (Isaiah. 26:20-21, Jeremiah in contending with the devil when he disputed about the body of Moses dared not bring against him a reviling accusation, buit said,"The Lord rebuke you!" 30:7, Matthew 24:21).

Isaiah 26:20.(NKJ) Come my people, enter your chambers, and shut your doors behind you:

> Hide yourself as it were for a little moment,
> Until the indignation is past.
> For behold the Lord comes out of His place
> To punish the inhabitants of the earth
> For their iniquity;
> The earth will also disclose her blood
> And will, no more, cover her slain.
> Jeremiah, 30:7(NKJ)

> Alas: For that day is great
> So that none is like it,
> And it is the time of Jacob's trouble
> But he shall be saved out of it.

This time of trouble is speaking of the great tribulation. Notice also, that the deliverance of those whose names were written in the Lamb's book (the book of the saved) is not before this time, but during.

To have your name written in the book means you are saved.

Daniel 12:2(NKJ) says, "And many of them that sleep in the dust of the earth shall awake, some to everlasting life and some to shame (and) everlasting contempt.

You can read a great deal more of this in Thessalonians 4:13-17.(NKJ) This Happens at the rapture, which occurs before the tribulation starts.

"But I do not want you to be ignorant, brethren concerning those who have fallen asleep, lest you sorrow as others who have no hope."

"For if we believe that Jesus died and rose again, so also which sleep in Jesus will God bring with him. For this we say to you by the Word of the Lord, that we which are alive (and) remain unto the coming of the Lord shall not prevent them which are asleep. For the Lord Himself shall descend from Heaven with a shout. With the voice of the archangel and with the trumpet of God the dead in Christ shall rise first. Then we which are alive and remain shall be caught up together with them in the clouds to meet the Lord in the air: And thus we shall always be with the Lord."

John 5:28-29.(NKJ) Do not "marvel at this, for the hour is coming in which all that are in the graves will hear His voice and come forth; those that have done good unto the resurrection of life, and those that done evil unto the resurrection of condemnation."

Those of faith will rise to eternal life, and when the rapture occurs the tribulation will begin. After the seven years of tribulation there will be two resurrections: the righteous to everlasting life for those who refused the mark, and the unrighteous to everlasting contempt (This is the White Throne Judgment). Jesus is the judge of all the earth. Then Jesus separates them into those receiving everlasting life at His right. Those on the left are doomed for all eternity. Matthew 25:46 says, and these shall go away into everlasting punishment, but the righteous into eternal life. This is referring to the time of judging all nations (Matthew 25:46).

Matthew 25:31-34.(NKJ) When the Son of Man shall come in His glory and all the holy angels with Him, then shall He sit upon the throne of His glory." He shall separate them one from another as a shepherd divides his sheep from the goats (Daniel 12:3) Living Bible. This is speaking of being wise unto salvation (Matthew 13:43). (NKJ) Then the righteous will shine forth as the sun in the kingdom of their Father. He who hath ears to hear, let him hear! 12:4. This time is Daniel's 70th week, which is the tribulation. World knowledge is at an all-time high right now. Freeways, air travel – we have no problem - seeing people running *to and fro*. This message was not for Daniel's time. His book was sealed. The 12th chapter of Daniel looks into the future. The Book of Daniel is easier understood today than ever before - perhaps because we are living in the time of the end. Is this the age of the coming of the Lord? The back and forth and *to and fro* refers to the movement of a person searching for something. In the tribulation, people will search for answers to the devastation.

Daniel 5.(NKJ) *Then I, Daniel, looked, and behold, there stood two others, the one on this side of the bank of the river and the other on that side of the bank of the river.* These two are probably angel beings. Had the Lord wanted us to know their names He would have given them. The message is the important thing. The message carrier is not important. The bank of the river is not important – it could have been the Tigris. The fact that there were two is for witnessing for by two, a thing is established. The two could also symbolize the spiritual house of Israel and the physical Israel.

Daniel 12:6.(NKJ) And one said to the man clothed in linen which was upon the waters of the river, "How long shall it be to the end of these wonders?"

Linen stands for righteousness. The man clothed in linen was of a higher rank of the two men. They were looking to Him for answers, as if He were the Lord. Notice also, that he was on the water, not in the water. We see in the following scripture that the disciples asked the Lord Jesus the same question.

Matthew 24:3(NKJ). "Now as he sat upon the Mount of Olives, the disciples came unto Him privately, saying, "Tell us when will these things be? And what shall be the sign of your coming and of the end of the age?" When most people look at the Lord, they see the figure of a man. It could also be Michael representing the Lord Jesus. We also see someone similar to this in Chapter 10:5.

Daniel 12:7(NKJ).Then *I heard the man clothed in linen which was upon the waters of the river, when he held up his right hand and his left hand unto heaven, and swore by Him who liveth forever, that it shall be for a time, times, and a half; and when he shall have accomplished to scatter the power of the holy people, all these things shall be finished.*

This is speaking of the three-and-one half year period of time, is one-year, then times two years, and a half time is half a year. The following scriptures speak of the same thing.

Revelation 10:5-6(NKJ). *The angel whom I saw standing on the sea and on the land raised up his hands to heaven. and swore by Him who lives forever and ever, who created heaven and the things that are in it and the earth and the things that are in it, and the sea and the things that are in it that there should be delay no longer. He that liveth forever and ever is*

God, it is the power of the holy people. This could be the time when God pours out His Spirit on all flesh.

One of the basic principles of warfare that is centuries old, is that an army kept together can defeat a larger army that is separated. Now Daniel's strange words make sense. The power of the holy people is already scattered which, when completed, will make our very survival impossible on any merely human basis, nothing but the power of God can rescue us. Yet, in all this there is hope. That is exactly what brings God to the rescue, for the angel told Daniel, *when he shall have accomplished to scatter the power of the holy people, all these things shall be finished.*

Daniel 12:8(Living Bible). *I heard what he said but I did not understand what he meant. So* asked how will all this finally end my lord?" Daniel is like us. He heard the words, but he did not understand what they were saying. His only chance of understanding is the Lord.

Daniel 12:9. And he said, *Go your way, Daniel, for the words are closed up and sealed till the time of the end.* The words are sealed until the time of the end. These things will become more apparent to the generation that this comes upon. I personally believe this is our generation. The reading of the book of Daniel was not sealed, but the understanding was sealed.

Daniel 12:10(NKJ) *Many shall be purified and made white, and refined; but the wicked shall do wickedly: and none of the wicked shall understand; but the wise shall understand.*

Salvation will come to pass to many Jews during the Great Tribulation. Zachariah 13:8-9NKJ) says, *And it shall come to pass in all the land,"Says the Lord,"That two-thirds in it shall be cut off and die,But one-third shall be left in it: I will bring the one-third through the fire,Will refine them as silver is refined,And test them as gold is tested. They will call on My name, And I will answer them.I will say, This is My people'; And each one will say, The Lord is my God.'"*

The truly saved develop in godliness through trials. The unsaved pursue false values, but true wisdom comes from God. Only those who belong to God will understand. The blood of the Lord Jesus purifies the christian. We are made white because we have been washed in His blood.

Revelation 7:14 (NKJ)says, and I said unto him, sir you know. So he said to me: *These are the ones who came out of great tribulation and have their robes, and made them white in the blood of the Lamb.*

John 16:33.*(NKJ) These things I have spoken to you that in Me you may have peace in the world, you will have tribulation; but be of good cheer, I have overcome the world.*

The wicked live now. They do not look to the eternity.

Daniel 12:11. *And from the time that the daily sacrifice shall be taken away and the abomination of desolation set up, there shall be one thousand two hundred and ninety days."*

This is where all worship will be stopped. This reference is to the end daily temple sacrifice, previously allowed under the covenant with the Antichrist formed with Israel. This happens in the middle of the last 7 years.

Daniel 12:12. (NKJ)*Blessed is he that waits and comes to the thousand three hundred and five and thirty -five days.*

The christians are blessed. The vials of God's judgment will be poured out upon all the anti-christian states. The enemies of Christ will be destroyed. Making ready for this kingdom, happy is the man that will be found waiting for these times and live to enjoy them.

Daniel 12:13.(NKJ) *But you go your way till the end, for you shall, and will arise to your inheritance at the end of the days"* Daniel would not live to see the fulfillment of his own prophecies, but is promised that he would be resurrected to receive his reward (thou shall stand in thy lot). All who trust in Daniel's God will likewise be blessed.

Luke 21:36(NKJ). *Watch therefore and pray always that you may be counted worthy to escape all things that shall come to pass, and stand before the Son of Man.* Every person will stand before Jesus to be judged. Those who did not receive Jesus as Savior will be judged guilty, sent to the lake of fire to everlasting torment.

As christians we will all receive everlasting life. We are going to jump into the stealth rider, go up over the mountain pass, go down the other side, go past Ezekiel 36 and 37, down through the valley, go past the Tigris River and camp at the gold mines of Ezekiel 38, 39, camp there and search the riches of God's words of End Time prophecies.

Isaiah. 42:9(Living Bible). *We have to remember that everything prophesied has come true, and now I will prophesy again. I will tell you the future before it happens.*

Chapter 9

Invaders from The North:

A few months ago, I was watching, I believe it was 60 Minutes. They were interviewing Israeli Prime Minister, Benjamin Netanyahu, and how it fits in with End Time Prophecy. God's been bringing Israelis back to the land of Israel from all over the world. For years it was desolate and barren. But now Israel is a luscious green oasis, very fertile, one of the top producers of produce. They struck oil on the Golan Heights. They are a leader in commerce and technology, just as the Lord said in his Word would happen in the last days. So, this sets up what Ezekiel prophesied some 2500 years ago. So, lets unlock the treasures of God's prophetic Word of the End of Days. Let's dig deep and see what the riches of Ezekiel 38-39 say. Let's bring in the excavators, so we can get down to the treasures of God's Word and find the archives of Ezekiel's prophetic writings.

On May 14th 1948, Israel became a nation. This is when the prophetic time clock was set in motion. On this date, Israel did not possess Jerusalem — that did not come until the war of 1967. This was fulfilled Bible prophecy, because Jerusalem plays a significant role in end time prophecy. The Arab world believes Jerusalem belongs to the Palestinians. But that will never happen because God made a promise that this land belongs to Israel.

The Bible dares to predict the future hundreds of times – the prophecies that have been fulfilled, and the ones that are coming. God lives in the Eternal realm, so nothing is too hard for Him. As His Word tells us, a day is like a thousand years and a thousand years is like a day. Luke 21:20(Living Bible) says, *And when you see Jerusalem surrounded by armies, then you will know that the time of its destruction has arrived.* Jerusalem is the center of the events to come.

Ezekiel 37:1(Living Bible) *The Lord gave this old Prophet this prophetic word. The Lord took hold of me, and I was carried away by the Spirit of the Lord to a valley filled with bones. He led me all around among the bones that covered the valley floor. They were scattered everywhere across the ground and were completely dried out. Then He asked me "Son of man, can these bones become living people again?" O Sovereign Lord, I replied. You alone know the answer to that.*

Then the Lord told Ezekiel to preach a sermon to these dry bones (V.4). Then he said, speak a prophetic message to these bones and say, "Dry bones listen to the word of the Lord! This is what the Sovereign Lord says! *Look, I am going to put breath into you and make you live again! I will put flesh and muscle on you and cover you with skin. I will put breath into you, and you will come to life. Then, you will know I am the Lord"*

So, I spoke this message just as he told me. Suddenly, as I spoke, there was a rattling noise all across the valley. The bones of each body came together and attached themselves as complete skeletons. Then as I watched, muscles and flesh formed over the bones. Then skin formed to cover their bodies, but they had no breath in them.

Then he said to me, "Speak a prophetic message to the winds, Son of man. Speak a prophetic message and say, "This is what the Sovereign Lord says! come, breath, from the far winds! Breathe into these dead bodies so they may live again."

So, I spoke the message as he commanded me and breath came into their bodies so they may live again. They all came to life and stood up on their feet – a great army.

Then he said to me, "Son of man these bones represent the people of Israel. They are saying we have become old dry bones – all hope is gone. Our nation is finished. Therefore, prophesy to them and say, this is what the sovereign Lord says. O my people, I will open your graves of exile and cause you to rise again. Then I bring you back to the land of Israel. When this happens, O my people, you will know that I am the Lord. I will put my Spirit in you and you will live again and return home to your land. Then you will know that I am the Lord and I have spoken and I have done what I said. Yes, the Lord has spoken."

Now let's tunnel down to chapters 38-39. We can look as the Lord gives this prophecy of the last days (38.1).

38.1(Living Bible). This is another message the Lord gave to Ezekiel 2500 years ago. The Lord said to Ezekiel to face Gog in the land of Magog.

38:15.(Living Bible) You will come from your homeland in the distant north with your vast calvary and your mighty army.

39:2(Living Bible). I will turn you around and drive you toward the mountains of Israel, bringing you from the distant north. When God said this to Ezekiel, regarding Gog and Magog, look at a map. What God is showing us furthest north is Russia. The Lord says in 38:3, Give him the message of prophesy against him. Give him this message from the Sovereign Lord. The Lord said I am your enemy ("Uh, oh", this isn't going to end well). I will turn you around and put hooks in your jaws. When you have a stubborn horse, an insubordinate horse, you would put a bridle in the horse's mouth that has these hooks. It would dig into the horse's jaw, and you can guide the horse where you want. In this situation, and the situations with us, God is leading – whether any of us want to believe it or not.

So, here we have this coalition headed up by Russia and this gathering of Muslim nations. They will invade Israel from all sides. God names them in Ezek. 38:5(Living Bible) Persia, which is modern day Iran, Turkey, Ethiopia, which is Sudan, and Libya. Right now, Russia has its footprint all over the Middle East. Whoever is reading this now can see these things happening. There is Russia propping up the regime of Asad. Syria has a treaty with Iran. Turkey, Russia and Iran have a treaty with Libya. Scientists from Iran have visited Russian scientists on many occasions regarding nuclear power. The hatred for Israel and the United States is so prevalent, that they call us big Satan and Israel little Satan. Then it says in 38:6, that there is Beth-tog Armah from the distant north and many others. God is aligning these nations as we sit here today. All of these forces will come down through the mountains of Israel with their weaponry.

Let's read what God's Word says in 38:7(LivingBible). Get ready; be prepared! Keep all the armies around you mobilized and take command of them. A long time from now, you will be called into action. In the distant future (this was written 2500 years ago – it is not as distant as when Ezekiel wrote these prophetic words), you will swoop down on the land of Israel, which will be enjoying peace after recovering from war, and after its people have returned from many lands to the mountains of Israel. You will say that Israel is unprotected land, filled with unwalled villages! I will march against her and destroy these people who live in such confidence!

At the beginning of the 7-year tribulation, in the first three-and-a-half years, the Antichrist is going to make this false treaty. He is going to help them build their temple. This is a false security. They will have no one to back them up. In the U.S. today, this administration is in alliance with Israel. But this country is so divided. There is so much hatred. At this time there will be nobody. In Genesis 12:3,(Living Bible) God told Abraham, I will bless those who bless you, and I will curse him who curses you; and in you all the families of the earth shall be blessed. The bottom line is that it is irrelevant. God has their back.

As soon as this massive army crosses into Israel (look out!), the Lord is going to take control. He has been controlling things all along. Just as in Exodus, when Pharoah came down on Moses and the Israelites trapped at the Red Sea, Pharoah mocked God by saying that their God is a poor planner. The end result - Pharoah and his army were wiped out. The end result for this massive army – wiped out – demolished. We must always remember that God has our backs. Deut. 32:35 says, Vengeance is mine and recompense (make amends – payback). Their foot shall slip in due time; for the day of their calamity is at hand, and the things to come hasten upon them.

What about America? In prophecy, you see the main players mentioned here. What about the U.S.? God wants to get our attention! Deut. 28. However, if you do not obey the Lord our God and do not care to follow all his commands and decrees that I am giving you today, all these curses will come upon you and overtake you. You will be cursed in the city and cursed in the country.

There are going to be natural disasters, the insurance companies call them acts of God, eroding society. We are heading for a cashless society - John spoke of it in 96 A.D. There is also the mark of the beast – no man will be able to buy or sell without this mark.

Countries around the world are banning their high notes. Australia – Citibank got rid of their ATM machines; Sweden – 20 percent of their purchases were cash; Singapore – no cash. The Bible is two-thirds prophecy. Like I said, earlier – where is the U.S.? In Ezekiel 38, 39. There is Russia, Iran, naturally, Israel, Turkey, Baltic states, Libya, Ethiopia. Where is America? There is a company in

Wisconsin that wants to put a chip in peoples' hand. Three market squares, 1 for convenience - the long-planned scam to record every transaction and make it possible to function. They can come and go with just their hand, turn their computer on with just their hand.

Israel is the center of all this, and is the size of Connecticut. It is the center geographically of all the land masses of the Earth. In the valley of Megiddo, there is a Norad center, a central command where Armageddon is going to be fought. We are founded on God's Word, but we've fallen away from the Lord. We've stood beside Israel since the inception. We cannot accept the blessing without accepting the curses.

The seven curses in Deut. 28. There is a decline in church attendance here in the U.S. In 1994 it was 68 percent; in 2014 it was 49 percent. We can see America eroding away. The first curse in Deuteronomy is madness (28:28). *The Lord shall smite them with madness and blindness and astonishment of heart.* There are demonic madness killings in schools, suicide is off the charts, 150,000 involved in gang violence in the U.S. – just in Chicago. Many are hooked on drugs due to the opioid epidemic. There are 274 million opioid prescriptions written per year. We're watching the young and old die each year. 100,000 people will die this year from a drug overdose. Twice as many as car deaths. It's a curse. Satan is in the middle of it. Depression is now highly prevalent in our society.

The second is the curse of drought, Deut. 28:22-24.(Living Bible) The Lord will strike you with wasting diseases, fever and inflammation, with scorching heat and drought, and with blight and mildew. These disasters will pursue you until you die. The skies above will be as unyielding as bronze, and the earth beneath will be as hard as iron. The Lord will change the rain that falls on your land into powder and dust that will pour down from the sky until you are destroyed.

You might say that we are now in a drought. The secular world says it's global warming. Here, the State of Colorado is in drought condition. 50 percent of the states in America are in drought condition. God is giving us warning, here in the United States, as well as the rest of the world, with this coronavirus pandemic. The total deaths due to the pandemic has surpassed 250,000 world-wide. We need to wake up! There was the West Nile virus, Aids in the 1980s and 90s, Ebola, bird flu, H1N1, Zika.

The fourth curse says that you shall betroth a wife but another man shall lie with her. You shall build a house, but you shall not dwell in it. These verses have to do with the destruction of the family unit – divorce, adultery, the abandonment of the home. In the 1960s only 8 percent of the population were single parents raising their children. Today, this number has grown to 30 percent.

In the days of Noah, and Sodom and Gomorrah, they did not have Bibles. What is our excuse in the days we live in? In addition, the thing today is to cohabitate. I stand guilty before you, Lord, on this living together before marriage.

This happened back when Jesus visited the Samaritan woman at the well in John Chapter 4. Jesus and his disciples stopped at a well at the village of Sycar. Jesus was tired from a long walk. It was about noontime and Jesus was alone, as his disciples had gone into the village to buy food. A woman came from the city to get water, like she did every day. Jesus asked her for a drink.

John 4:7.(LIving Bible) Let's pick up the story from here. "Please give me a drink." The woman was surprised that he asked her for a drink. "You are a Jew and I am a Samaritan woman. Why are you asking me for a drink?" Then Jesus said to her, "If you only knew the gift God has for you and who you are, speaking to you, you would ask me and I would give you living water." Anyone who drinks this water will soon become thirsty again. But those who drink the water

I give will never be thirsty again. It becomes a fresh, pulsing spring within them, giving them eternal life (being born again). Then the woman said, give me this water! Then I'll never be thirsty again, and I won't have to come here to get water.

"Go get your husband" (here it is). I don't have a husband. Jesus said, "You're right. You don't have a husband, for you have had five husbands and you aren't even married to the man you're living with now. You certainly spoke the truth. Jesus said to her, you Samaritans know very little about the one you worship, while the Jews know all about him for salvation comes through the Jews (through Jesus). The woman said, I know the Messiah is coming – the one who is called the Christ (interesting statement). When he comes, he will explain everything to us. Then Jesus told her, "I Am the Messiah." Then the disciples returned.

The woman left her water jar and went back to the city and told the people of the city, "Come and see a man who told me everything I ever did. Could he possibly be the Messiah?" So, the people came streaming from the village to see him.

Verse 39. Many Samaritans from the village believed in Jesus because the woman had said, "He told me everything I ever did." When they came out to see him, they begged him to stay in their village, so he stayed for two days – long enough for many more to hear his message and believe. Then they said to the woman, "Now we believe - not just because of what you told us, but because we have heard him ourselves. Now we know that he is the Savior of the world."

Each and every one of us has to come to this realization. We must repent and ask for forgiveness of our sins - ask the Lord into our lives. As far as the U.S. and us, if we do not do that, Judgment and destruction awaits all of us. Jesus said in Math. 24:22,(LivingBible) in fact, unless that time of calamity is shortened, not a single person will survive. The fate for the U.S. is the same as in the days of Noah, and the days of Sodom and Gomorrah. There will be no hope.

We see that Russia and these masses will come down upon Israel. They want something – oil - something of the wealth of Israel, as they are becoming very prosperous. This army is going to be mobile and very agile. Ezekiel used horses – that's all he knew. Islam has infiltrated these regions and these countries mentioned in these prophecies.

So, the Lord has set these things in motion – lining things up. 38:7. Get ready, be prepared! It says a long time from now will be the last days. In the distant future God is speaking of Russia. You and your allies, a vast and awesome army, will roll down on them like a storm and cover the land like a cloud.

Verse 10. This is what the Sovereign Lord says: At that time evil thoughts will come to your mind and you will devise a wicked scheme. God said this is his land. He says, thus I will magnify Myself and sanctify Myself and I will be known in the eyes of many nations. Then they shall know that I am the Lord.

The world today hates Israel. God said in Ezek. 38:17, I have spoken in former days to my servants – Prophets of Israel. Who prophesied for years in those days that I would bring you against them? Israel is living securely. God is telling, you should know this – I protect them. V.16, I will bring you against my land. It is not Israel's land or the Palestinian's land – it is God's land. Just as Russia and the countries with them, and the United States, walk blindly toward destruction. They have turned away from Israel. The Lord says there shall be a great earthquake – not just an earthquake, it says a great earthquake – off the Richter scale in Israel; so that the fish of the sea, the birds of the heavens, the beasts of the field, all creeping things that creep on the earth, and all men who are on the earth. God is going to cause these alliances to turn on themselves.

This has happened before. I will punish you and your armies with disease and bloodshed. I will send torrential rain and hailstones, fire and burning sulfur.

The United States detonated the world's first thermonuclear weapon, the hydrogen bomb, on Eniwetok, in the Pacific. The test gave the United States advantage over the Soviet Union. It was the next stage of atomic weaponry – a thermonuclear bomb. This new weapon was approximately 1,000 times more powerful than the conventional nuclear devices. They had ships anchored there to see what damage would be done. The most damage was done on the top of these ships. The tremendous heat was at the center of this blast; with a mushroom cloud compressing the atmosphere, where it is extremely cold. The moisture from this bomb would cause hailstones, up to two hundred pounds in weight, causing damage to these ships. Then the Lord said, you will fall in the open fields. I will rain down fire on Magog. Not only will there be this devastation, but the Lord is going to rain down fire on Russia and on its allies, on their own land. There it is – the end result. 39:.6, *Then they will know that I am the Lord.*

Verse 7. *In this way I will make known my Holy Name along with my people of Israel. I will not let anyone bring shame on it. And the nations, too, will know that I am the Lord, the Holy One of Israel (Jesus). That day of judgment will happen just as I declared it (Just as it was written).*

Then the people in the towns of Israel will go out and pick up their small and large shields, bows and arrows, javelins and spears, and they will use them for fuel. There will be enough to last them seven years! It will take seven months for the people of Israel to bury the bodies and cleanse the land. Everyone in Israel will help, for it will be a glorious victory for Israel when I demonstrate my glory on that day, says the Sovereign Lord.

After seven months, teams of men will be appointed to search the land for skeletons so the land will be made clean again. Here is something interesting: whenever bones are found, a marker will be set up so that the burial crews will take them to be buried.

What this could be is the result of radiation from nuclear weapons and the fallout. Could this be God's way of bringing destruction upon this massive army? God rained down fire and brimstone on Sodom and Gomorrah. Zechariah 14:12 (Living Bible)has the result of nuclear fallout. And the Lord will send a plague on all the nations that fought against Jerusalem. Their people will become like walking corpses, their flesh rotting away. Their eyes will rot in their sockets and their tongues will rot in their mouths. On that day they will be terrified – stricken by the Lord with great panic.

Well, Lord, this journey is complete. It has been an adventure through the End Time Prophecies. Thank you for guiding me through, Lord. Your Holy Spirit was with me on this excursion through God's Holy Word, down the rough terrain, through the riches that laid beneath the surface – the richness of wealth that was buried. From where I started to the end, Father, it's been a real adventure. Lord, from Everlasting to Everlasting, you are God.

I know plagiarism is a very serious thing. But Lord, just as Ruth gleaned the fields of Boaz, I gleaned the field of Your Word with the wisdom and knowledge of these men of God. Hal Lindsey, who has spent his life studying End Time Prophecy; Hal Lindsey Ministries; the late Chuck Smith Calvary Chapel, where I got saved 40 years ago. What can be said of Chuck? Greg Laurie – what God has done with this man's life; Harvest Church, Riverside, California; Harvest Crusades; Don Stewart – I remember Don through Calvary Chapel some 40 years ago; Chuck Misler – His wisdom far exceeds mine. Listening to Chuck – he's going to take you deep; Jon Coursen – Searchlight Ministries. He's the Lead Pastor Applegate Christian

Fellowship; David Jeremiah Turning Point Ministries Shadow Mountain Church; Jeff Kinley.

Let's head back to where it started, Lord. The Mount of Olives with the disciples, to where you are coming back, and take an adventure through the Book of Revelations.

Chapter 10

The Treasures of Our Lord Unveiled:

Revelation 1:1 The revelation of Jesus Christ the unveiling. This book is about our Lord which God gave to him to show unto his servants, things which must shortly come to pass and He sent and signified it by his angel unto his servant John. No other book in the Bible this book is given by God. We know that the word of God is God-breathed inspired by the Holy Spirit. The 20th century is when prophecy started to kick into gear people started studying. The angel told Daniel shut up the words and seal the book until the time of the end: and many shall run to and fro, and knowledge shall increase (Daniel 12:4).(NKJ)

John was the recipient of this commission by the Lord, of what he saw. God time traveled him to see these events. The Lord told him to write in a book what he saw. John was commissioned to do the impossible apart from the Holy Spirit. John was to write everything he saw, and could only use what he knew and saw in the first century. This is the church age, and John was told to write about these things. John wrote on several occasions throughout Revelation. Can we imagine what John was going through as he was writing these things? He had an encounter with a being led by the Holy Spirit in his writings of the Gospel of John, A. D. 90 to 95. Revelation was written around A.D. 96. Throughout this study we're going to see John.

I saw in 1ˢᵗ John(Living Bible) where he wrote in Verse 1, *We proclaim to you the one who existed from the beginning, whom we have heard and seen with our own eyes and touched him with our own hands. He is the Word of life. This One was life itself, He was revealed to us, and we have seen Him. And now we testify and proclaim to you that He is eternal life. He was with the Father and then He was revealed to us. We proclaim to you what we ourselves have actually seen and heard, so that you may have fellowship with us. Our fellowship is with the Father and with his son Jesus Christ. We are writing these things so that you may fully share our joy.*

We are currently living in the church age. This is covered in the first three chapters. He is to write this book in an outline form. John uses the phrases: I looked and behold, and I looked and heard. John was saying he was there. Verse 2. who faithfully reported everything he saw. This is his report of the Word of God and the testimony of Jesus Christ. Verse 3. This is the greatest blessing of this book. There is a blessing for us as we read and study it and obey what it says for the time is near (Interesting!). Verse 4, for grace and peace to you from the one who is, who always was, and who is still to come, from the Sevenfold Spirit before his throne and from Jesus Christ. He is the faithful witness to these things, the first to rise from the dead and the ruler of all kings of the world.

We can see the theme of this book the unveiling of our great God and Savior. All glory to him who loves us and has freed us from our sins by the shedding of his blood for us. He has made us a kingdom of priests. All glory and power to him forever and ever! Look! He comes with the clouds of heaven and everyone will see him, even those who pierced him and all the nations of the world will mourn for him, yes! Amen! I am the alpha and omega, the beginning and the end," says the Lord God. "I am the one who is who always was and who is still yet to come - the Almighty One.

John is told not to seal up this book. In Daniel he is told to seal up the book. We have to remember that Jesus and John had a special love for each other. John was in the Inner Circle with his brother James and Peter. When we see in Verse 4 the Sevenfold spirit, this is the Holy Spirit. He is the implementer (especially used for a particular purpose). The Holy Spirit is the one that carries things out before God the Father.

When we accept Jesus as our Savior, the Holy Spirit comes into our hearts and lives and reveals the truth of God's Word to us, and seals us as God's children. We have God the Father, the Holy Spirit and Jesus Christ with us. Jesus is the faithful witness to these things, the first to rise from the dead and the ruler of all the kings of the world. All glory to him who loves us and has freed us from our sins by the shedding of his blood. He has made us a kingdom of priests for God his Father. All glory and power to him forever and ever!

When Jesus' human body was hanging on the Roman cross, Jesus was holding the Deity together. He was God and man. Colossians 1:15(Living Bible) says, Christ is the visible image of the invisible God. He existed before anything was created and is supreme over all creation. For through him God created everything in the heavenly realms and on earth. He made the things we can see and the things we can't see, such as thrones, kingdoms, rulers, and authorities in the unseen world. Everything was created through him and for him. He existed before anything else and he holds all Creation together.

Christ is also the head of the church which is the body. He is - supreme over all who rise from the dead, so he is first and everything. God in all his fullness was pleased to live in Christ, and through him God reconciled everything to himself. He made peace with everything in heaven and on earth by means of Christ's blood on the cross. John 1:1(Living Bible), In the beginning was the Word (already existed), and the Word was with God and the Word was God. He existed in the beginning with God. God created everything through him and nothing was created except through him. The Word gave life to everything that was created. The one thing we have to remember about the Book of Revelation is that we have to try to decode these symbols that are used. We have to remember that God is not trying to conceal but to reveal.

Revelation is the last book in God's Word and we have to pray that God Reveals His Truth to us. This is a book that we have to dig deep into, but as we dig deep, the Truth of this book will be revealed to us as we dig up the treasures that God wants to unveil to us. Indescribable things, His truths. I think if we keep digging, we're going to hit the main vein of gold and the riches that await us. Lord, open our hearts and minds. We have to remember the unique promise of His Divine Blessing: blessed is the one who reads the words of this prophecy and blessed are those who hear it and take it to heart, what is written in it, because the time is near.

Here is a story by Max Lucado: An ancient legend tells us of the general whose Army was afraid to fight. The soldiers were frightened because the enemy was too strong. Its Fortress was high and its weapons were mighty. The King however was not afraid. He knew his men could win, but how could he convince them? He had an idea. He told his soldiers he possessed a magical coin - a coin which would foretell the outcome of the battle. On one side was an eagle and on the other side a bear. He would toss the coin, and if it landed eagle side up, they would win. If it landed with the bear up, they would lose. The Army was silent as the coin flipped in the air. The soldiers circled as it fell to the ground. They held their breath as they looked, and shouted when they saw the eagle. The Army would win. Bolstered by the assurance of the coin toss, the men marched against the castle and won. It was only after the victory that the king showed the men the coin. The two sides were identical. Though the story is fictional the truth is reliable: assured victory empowers the army.

This may be the reason God gives us the Book of Revelation. God shows us victory, and we the soldiers are privileged to have a glimpse into the final battlefield. All breaks loose as all Heaven comes forth, and the two collide in the ultimate battle of Good and Evil. Left standing amidst the smoke and thunder is the Son of God. Jesus, born in a manger, now triumphs over Satan. Satan is defeated, Christ is triumphant, and we the soldiers are assured of the victory: Let Us March! We have to remember that this is the unveiling. It's like an onion we have to peel black one layer at a time. We have to remember that John is writing this in A.D. 96, trying to describe things of the days we live in, or in the future that we don't even know about. 8. *I am the Alpha and Omega the beginning and the end says the Lord who is, who was, and who is to come - the Almighty!*

Let's outline this book: I - Introduction; 1-2 - Letters to the Seven Churches; 2-3 -Things to Come; 4-22A - The Heavenly Throne; B - The Seven Sealed Scrolls; 5C - Opening Six Seal; 6D - The Great Tribulation; 7E - Opening the Seventh Seal; 8F - The Fifth and Sixth Trumpet; 9G - Mighty Angel and a Scroll; 10H - Two Witnesses; 11I - The Seventh Trumpet; 11J - Seven key Persons; 12-15K - Bowls of God's Wrath; 16L - Fall of Babylon; 17-18M – Jesus' Second Coming; 19 N - Jesus Reign; 20O - Great White Throne Judgment; 20P - New Heaven and Earth; 21

In John, remember they say that he was boiled in oil, but it didn't harm him so they exiled him to the desolate island of Patmos. God wasn't through with John yet. John was cast into a time machine from the natural to the supernatural. Time is relative, as we counted it here on earth, but John said he was in the spirit, and he heard a loud voice behind him that sounded like a trumpet. Write what you see and send it to the seven churches, Ephesus, Smyrna, Pergamum, Thyatira, Sardis, Philadelphia, and Laodicea. In none of the Gospels did anyone ever described Jesus' features. We have no knowledge of what Jesus looked like. John saw Jesus in his glorified form. He was dressed in a long robe and he had a gold band around his chest. His head and hair were white like wool, as white as snow. Have you ever tried to put a face to a voice on the radio, and when you see them in person, he or she doesn't look anything like you imagined? John is not seeing Jesus the way he remembers Him. He knows it's the Lord, but his hair is as white as snow when he sees him in his Glorified state. The eyes that he looked into as he walked with the Master for three short years, are now as flames of fire, which indicates judgment. His feet were like bronze that glows in a hot furnace, which also means judgment. His voice was like flooding waters.

As christians, we can survey the world and really see how corrupt things are, but we know throughout history that we have a God that's always been in the shadows of history, and that he has a plan. We, as christians, are not to be disturbed by the chaos, violence, strife, and the threat of wars that fill our daily newspapers.

Every day we can see evidence of the fulfillment of Bible prophecy. We can see, like a chess game, that events are being pushed into position and that God has a plan. Job 12:10 says that our very breath is in his hands. No matter how bad things get, we know how the story ends. You might say, Ray, you are a pessimist. No, Mark 13:23 says. Watchout! I have warned you about all this ahead of time.

I believe Chuck Swindoll said this - *I'm just the newspaper boy throwing the papers.* None of us knows when our end is coming, and remember, as of the year 2015, 55 million people die each year.

Are you ready to look a righteous God in the eye? Jesus wants to forgive us of our sin. He wants to cleanse our hearts with his blood by what He did for us on the cross, and fill our lives with the Holy Spirit. Jesus said, *come to me and he that cometh to me I will in no wise cast out.* He held the Seven Stars in his right hand (power), and a sharp double-edged sword came out of his mouth (The Word of God) that judges all humanity. *I was dead but look I am alive forever and ever. And I hold the keys to death and to the place of the dead (Hell).* Jesus defeated Satan, death and Hell.

Verse 17. Remember, John saw him and fell down at his feet like a dead man. John was terrified when Jesus put his right hand on him. This signifies power. Then Jesus said, *don't be afraid, I am the First and the Last.* There is a christian song that I've heard along the way in life. It says, we must wait, wait, wait on the Lord. We must wait, wait, wait on the Lord. Learn our lessons well, and in his timing, he will tell us where to go, what to do and what to say? Here John is out on this little desolate island maybe wondering, now what? Never try to figure out God's plan. Just get ready for the adventure of your life, like John, when he was about to go on the ride of his life writing the last book of the Bible. It was the unveiling of his God and Savior and also his friend, who reveals the events leading up to the End of the Age.

Chapter 2: Write this to the angel of the Church of Ephesus. The One who holds the Seven Stars in his right hand and walks among the seven golden lamp stands. This is Jesus. He says, *I know thy works.* He says this of each church. These churches comprise church history. These churches exist today and they also have historical relevance. They have Jesus' return as coming quickly, but that didn't happen as time moved on, since it's been a long time.

Scoffers have come along, mocking - when is his coming? They've been saying this for years. The problem with these churches is the evil within. Jesus said this in the parable of the sower. Matthew 13.(Living Bible) The scattering of the seeds. Listen, a farmer went out to plant some seeds, and as he scattered them across the field, some seeds fell on a footpath and the birds came and ate them. Other seeds fell on shallow soil with underlying rock. The seeds sprouted quickly because the soil was shallow, but the plants soon wilted under the hot sun and since they didn't have roots, they died. Others seeds fell among thorns that grew up and choked out the tender plants. Still other seed fell on fertile soil, and they produced a crop that was thirty, sixty, and even a hundred times as much as had been planted. Anyone with ears to hear should listen and understand Verse 18.

Now listen to the explanation of the parable about the farmer planting seeds. The seed that fell on the footpath represents those who hear the message about the kingdom and don't understand that it is going to the evil one. Satan comes and snatches away the seed that was planted in their hearts. The seed on rocky soil represents those who hear the message and immediately receive it with joy, but since they don't have deep roots, they don't last long. They fall away as soon as they have problems or are persecuted for believing God's Word. The seed that fell among the thorns represents those who hear God's Word, but all too quickly the message is crowded by the worries of this life and the lure of wealth, so no fruit is produced. The seed that fell on good soil represents those who truly hear and understand God's Word and produce a harvest of thirty, sixty, or even a hundred times as much as had been planted.

We see this in Acts with the first church. Jesus ascended to the Father. The church received the Holy Spirit. Christ was at the center of spreading the Word of God to the known world. It spread like wildfire. Then Paul came along and wrote half of the New Testament. The church of Ephesus: We have to study God's Word – that's the personal application to our lives. The Holy Spirit put these churches in the book of prophecy and put them in order. Ephesus is the first church.

In the beginning of this letter there are the attributes of Jesus himself. There are certain formulas he uses for the churches. If they believe them, they could overcome the problems. Jesus always commends them for what they are doing right before he reprimands them. Thyatira gets nothing good said about them. Smyrna is not rebuked because of all the suffering they have endured. The other church that was not rebuked is Philadelphia. Ephesus had knowledge but they turned away from the Lord, their first love. Smyrna is the persecuted poor church but rich in the Lord. The church of Pergamum is the church that compromised with the world. The Roman Catholic Church started saying that there are not believers in the church. This is the beginning of not going to God directly, but putting a man between man and God. That spot is for Christ. The church of Thyatira became the great counterfeit church. I will repay each of you for what you have done. The Sardis church was filled with orthodoxy, rules and regiments, but not filled with the Spirit. Philadelphia was a church of revival mission evangelism with men of God like Whitefield and Wesley. It says I have put an open door before you which no one can shut. I know you have little strength, but you have obeyed my teachings and were not afraid to speak my name. I am coming soon. Continue strong in your faith so that no one will take away your crown. For Laodicea church, it says that they are neither cold nor hot. I'm ready to spit you out of my mouth. The literal translation is to vomit. Vomiting is the body's way of rejecting anything it cannot handle. God can't stand lukewarm faith. If God gave you a report card like the ones we received in school, how would ours read? We have to be honest with the Lord!

Chapter 4. What we have is a period from the church age to the transition period, when the church is caught up in the rapture. It says that after the vision of these things, *I looked and there before me was an open door in Heaven, and the same voice that spoke to me before with the sound of a trumpet said come up here.*

1Thes.4:15.(Living Bible) We tell you this directly from the Lord. We who are still living when the Lord returns will not meet him ahead of those who died. For the Lord himself will come down from Heaven with a commanding shout - with the voice of the Archangel and the trumpet call of God. First, the believers who have died will rise from their graves. Then together with them, we who are still alive and remain on the earth will be caught up in the clouds to meet the Lord. Then we will be with the Lord forever. Therefore, encourage each other with these words. Our bodies are made for this earth.

Let's read what Paul said in 1st Corinthians *15:50- 57(NKJ) Now this I say brethren, that flesh and blood cannot inherit the kingdom of God; nor does corruption inherit incorruption. Behold, I tell you a mystery: we shall not all sleep but we shall all be changed in a moment, in the twinkling of an eye at the last trumpet. For the trumpet will sound and the dead will be raised incorruptible and we will be changed. For this corruption must put on incorruption and this mortal must put on immortality. So, this corruptible has put on incorruption and this mortal has put on immortality, then shall be brought to pass the saying that is written: death is swallowed up in Victory. O death where is your sting? O Hades (hell) where is your victory? The sting of death is sin and the strength of sin is the law. But thanks be to God who gives us the victory through our Lord Jesus Christ.*

Verse 58(NKJ). Therefore, my beloved brethren, be steadfast unmovable, always abounding in the work of the Lord. You know that nothing you do for the Lord is ever useless.

In the throne we see the brilliance of God. John describes these precious stones, jasper and sardine stone (red). Also, before the throne there was something that looked like a sea of glass crystalline that gives off a purple hue. Paul told Timothy that God dwells in a light that is unapproachable by man. We only see the radiant light of the glory of God. It says that there was a rainbow encircling God's Throne. We usually only see a half a rainbow, but this rainbow made an entire circle. Imagine this, because someday we will see this sight. Around the throne there were 24 lesser thrones, and there were 24 elders that sat on these thrones. It said that there was one elder for each tribe of Israel. The other 12 were the apostles, and they had golden crowns on their heads and were clothed in white raiment. Out of the throne had come lightning and thundering and voices, and there had been seen lamps of fire burning before the throne.

We are told in Hebrews, that the Tabernacle Moses built in the wilderness, was actually a model of heavenly things, and the seven candlesticks were representative of the Holy Spirit. Next comes the cherubim, angelic beings created by God who seem to be the highest order of angels. Satan was one of these cherubim angels. He was perfect in beauty and knowledge, until iniquity filled him. Before the throne there was a sea of glass like unto crystal, and in the midst of the throne and round about the throne, four living creatures full of eyes in front and behind. The first living creature was like a lion, and the second was like a calf, and the third had the face of a man, and the fourth was a flying eagle. The cherubim angels were first mentioned in Genesis.

There are Bible scholars that we see in the four phases of Christ, represented in the four Gospels. The First, Matthew, presents Jesus as the lion of the tribe of Judah. The lion is known as the king of the beasts. The second was like a calf. Mark presents Jesus as the suffering servant, and the ox is considered the leader of the domesticated animals. The third was like a man. Luke presents Jesus as the Son of Man and the crowning order of God's creation. The fourth was like an eagle, and John presents Jesus as the Son of the Living God as the eagle being the greatest of the flying foul.

Satan was one of the anointed cherubim. Around the throne of God and their worship of Him, the four living creatures gave glory, honor and thanks to him that sat on the throne and who liveth forever and ever, the Eternal God. The four and 24 elders fell down before him to worship Him, and they cast their crowns before the throne. Thou art worthy, Lord, to receive glory and honor and power, for thou hath created all things for thy pleasure. There is the first scene in Heaven – the Throne of God, the cherubim about the throne and the worship of God upon the throne. This is probably going to be one of the first observations.

It is also important to accept that we were created for God's pleasure. This means that we should seek to please God. The interesting thing is that when we live to seek God, we have fulfillment in our lives. Matthew 7:7(NKJ) says, ask and it will be given to you, seek and you will find, knock and it will be opened to you. For everyone who asks receives and he who seeks finds, and to he who knocks it will be opened. Matthew 6:19,(NKJ) Do not lay up your treasures on earth where moth and rust destroy, and where thieves break in and steal, but lay up for yourselves treasures in heaven, where neither moth nor rust destroys and thieves do not break in and steal. For where your treasure is there your heart will be also. Matthew 10:39:(NKJ) If any man seeks to save his life, he's going to lose it, and he who loses his life for My sake will find it. If we really want to find what living is all about, we have to worship God while we are here on earth. We have to repent of our sins and ask Jesus to forgive our sins, then the Holy Spirit will come into our lives. Matthew 6:24(NKJ): No one can serve two masters, for either he will hate the one and love the other or else he will be loyal to the one and despise the other. You cannot serve God and mammon (the world). As we finish Chapter 4 with this scripture verse, we will use this as a prelude to Chapter 5.

In Chapter 5 we see that God created the heavens and the earth, and God gave it to man. Adam forfeited it to Satan in the Garden of Eden, when he chose to disobey God. The Lord told Adam and Eve not to eat of the tree, but they disobeyed and suffered death – separation from the Lord – and that's how it started. We have choices too, like Adam and Eve, but to walk with the Lord we have to swim against the current. It's easy to go with the current of the world. That is why Jesus came to redeem the world back to God. Matthew 4:1 says that when Jesus was out in the wilderness to be tempted by the enemy, Satan took Jesus onto a high mountain and showed him all the kingdoms of the world. He said to Jesus, I will give these all to you and the glory of them if you will bow down and worship me. They are mine and I can give them to whoever I will. Jesus did not dispute this claim, the world is in Satan's control, and when we receive Jesus Christ as our Savior, we become aliens to the world. You are not of the world. This world belongs to Satan, and Satan is in rebellion against God. Man has joined in this rebellion. Peter said we are redeemed not with corruptible things like silver and gold from our empty manner of living, but with the precious blood of Jesus Christ who was slain as a lamb without spot or blemish.

In 1st Peter 1:18 and19, Matthew 13:44,(NKJ) Jesus said the Kingdom of Heaven is like unto a man going through a field and discovering a treasure, *and who for the joy thereof immediately goes out and sells everything that he might buy the field so that he can obtain the treasure.* In this Parable the field is the world. Jesus gave everything to purchase the world. He gave his own life. For what purpose did he purchase the world? He purchased the world that he might take the treasure out of it. What is the treasure? His church - the body of Christ - for everyone who comes to believe and trust in him. We have the scene in heaven when God the Father is on the throne and there is a scroll in His right hand. Then an angel proclaimed with a strong, loud voice - who is worthy to open the scroll and loose the seal? No man was found worthy, no man has the capacity to redeem the world.

This thought was too much for John to bear and he begins to sob convulsively with the thought that Satan would forever have the world under his control. Then one of the elders told John to weep not: behold, The Lion of the tribe of Judah, the root of David, has prevailed to open the book and loose the seven seals. When John sees Jesus, he sees him as a lamb that had been slaughtered. Perhaps Jesus is still bearing the marks of the cross and his suffering for us. We might have the same shocking experience. When Jesus rose from the dead, Mary was there in the garden. She didn't recognize him. She thought he was the gardener. Remember that, when Jesus walked with the two disciples on the road to Emmaus, they didn't recognize him until he went in to eat dinner with them. When Jesus went to break bread they recognized him, probably because they saw his nail-pierced hands.

Then there was Thomas. When Jesus first appeared to the disciples that were gathered, Thomas wasn't there. They told Thomas what happened and he said he would not believe it unless he could put his finger in the hole in his hand and put his hand in his side. Then Jesus appeared again to them. This time Thomas was with them. Jesus said to him: Put your finger here and look at my hands put your hand into the wound in my side. Don't be faithless any longer "Believe!" Then Thomas said "My Lord and my God!" remember that Jesus was in his glorified body.

In Luke 24:37(Living Bible), the entire group was startled and frightened, thinking they were seeing a ghost. Jesus asked them at the beginning of this paragraph, why are you frightened why are your hearts filled with doubt? Look at my hands, look at my feet, you can see that it's really me. Touch me and make sure that I am not a ghost because ghosts don't have bodies, and you see that I do. In Isaiah 52 and 53, many as looked upon him were astonished. They were shocked. You could not recognize him as a human being, as he was marred. Remember, they covered his head and we're hitting him with their fists, "but He was wounded for our transgressions and bruised for our iniquities." He paid the price for our redemption. We could be very shocked when we first see Jesus. And when he had taken the book (the title deed to the earth), the four cherubim living creatures and 24 Elders fell down before the Lamb, having every one of them harps and golden vials full of odors, which are the prayers of the Saints. Revelations 5:8(NKJ) Mathew 6:10 says: *Your Kingdom come Your will be done on earth as it is in heaven.* Soon God's kingdom will be coming and soon God's will, will be done on earth as it is in heaven.

When Jesus comes and establishes his kingdom, we will see the earth as God intended.Revelation 5:9 (NKJ) And they sang a new song saying: *Your worthy to take the scroll and to open the seals, . For you were slain and you redeemed us to God by your blood, out of every tribe and tongue, people and nations.* Revelation 5—9 states, one in Christ.

Chapter 11

The Tribulation Begins:

In Chapter 6, the church is in heaven, declaring the worthiness of the Lamb to take the scroll and lose the seals. Revelation 5:11(NKJ) says:Then *I Looked and I heard the voice of many angels around the throne the living creatures and the elders and the number of them was ten thousand times ten thousand times thousands thousands. Worthy is the Lamb who was slain to receive power and riches and wisdom, and strength and honor and glory and blessing. And then I heard every creature which is in heaven and on earth and under the earth and in the sea, and they sang: Blessing and honor and glory and power Belong to the One sitting on the throne \And to the Lamb forever and ever* ! Then the four living beings said "Amen" and the 24 Elders fell down and worshiped the Lamb.

So, in Chapter 5 we got a glimpse into heaven. Jesus took the Scroll out of the Father's hand and now Jesus is about to break the seals chapter 6 The Four Horsemen of the Apocalypse. The first is the white horse - the Antichrist masquerading as Jesus (anti means against). We see the Antichrist coming onto the scene wearing a crown. Then we see in Revelation 19, the Lord Jesus. Then I saw heaven opened and a white horse was standing there. Its rider was named Faithful and True, for he judges fairly and wages a righteous

War. His eyes were like flames, and on him was a name that no one understood except himself. He wore a robe dipped in blood and His title was the Word of God.

Revelation 6 parallels Matthew 24, and we're getting the big picture. The Antichrist initiates war and Jesus, in chapter 19, is coming to put an end to war. So, the first thing we see is the white horse and this is the Antichrist - the false Messiah, the false Christ. The church is gone. The Antichrist begins to conquer the earth, bringing it under his power and control. At the center of this is Satan. He is still in control of this world.

In Revelation chapter 13, Satan gives his throne and authority to the Antichrist. According to Paul in 2nd Thessalonians, the Antichrist cannot come forth until the church is out of the way. *For that which hinders shall hinder until taken out of the way, and then shall the Son of Perdition be revealed.* The one that hinders is the Holy Spirit. The church is the only preserving factor in the world. Even the United States would be down the tubes. When the christians are gone, the world is going to say it was those christians that kept us from all the prosperity and everything else.

When the lamb broke the second seal, I heard the second living being say come, then another horse appeared - a red one. Its rider was given a mighty sword and the authority to take peace from the earth, and there was war and slaughter everywhere. In World War I, 10 people million lost their lives. In World War II there were 50 million deaths. What is the great sword? I believe the Lord is just going to let it happen. What I've read from other men of God who have studied this, and what I believe also, is that this means nuclear weapons.

Following Jesus' opening of the third seal is famine - perhaps a result of the use of nuclear weapons. It is said that there are approximately 23000 nuclear missiles. Even the rogue nations like

India and Pakistan have nuclear weapons. It says that one fourth of the world's population will be destroyed. There are approximately 7.5 to 8 billion people on the earth, so we're talking around two billion people. One nuclear submarine carries nuclear weapons in those warheads that are 40 times more powerful than the bombs dropped in World War II. "STOP" just think of that! 1Thessalonians 5:1(NKJ) says, But concerning the times and the seasons brethren you have no need that I should write to you, for you yourselves know perfectly that the day of the Lord so comes as a thief in the night. For when they say peace and safety, sudden destruction comes upon them as labor pains upon a pregnant woman, And they shall not escape, But you brethren are not in darkness so that this day should overtake you as a thief. You are all sons of light and sons of the day. We are not of the night nor of darkness, Therefore let us not sleep as others do, But let us watch and be sober, for those who sleep, sleep at night and those who get drunk, get drunk at night. But let us, who are of the day, be sober, putting on the breastplate of faith and love and as a helmet, the hope of salvation.

For God did not appoint us to wrath, but to obtain salvation through our Lord Jesus Christ, who died for us that whether we are awake or sleep, we should live together with Him.

So, the third horse unleashes the famine which follows the war. Could this be from a nuclear holocaust? One of the by-products could be a tremendous fallout which would destroy crops, which could change the atmosphere, and from which, as we'll see as we get into this further, there will be tremendous heat. Things will be so bad that it will cost a day's wage for a loaf of bread.

We see the next seal, and the horse was a pale green color which represents death, and hell follows a tremendous amount of death. We can see, if we jump to the last two paragraphs of this chapter, that the world will know that God's judgments have come.

Let's look at that a little closer. Then everyone, the kings of the earth, the rulers and the generals, the wealthy and the powerful, and every slave and free person, all hid themselves in the caves and among the rocks of the mountains, and cried out, fall on us and hide us from the face of the one who sits on the throne, and from the wrath of the Lamb. For the great day of their wrath has come and who is able to survive?

There is nothing more to say. Can we imagine the fear that is within these people, asking the mountains and the rocks to fall on them? They want to die, and we are only in the sixth chapter. Pretty frightening, and believe me, we couldn't even imagine these events. Let's go back to the 5th seal where these martyrs were at this time, and to all those who heard God's Word and didn't accept Christ as their Savior. Maybe you've witnessed, also, that they gave their lives to the Lord and died as martyrs. Then they shouted to the Lord and said, O Sovereign Lord holy and true how, long before you judge the people who belong to this world and avenge our blood for what they have done to us? Then a white robe was given to each of them, and they were told to rest a little longer until the full number of their brothers and sisters, their fellow servants of Jesus who were to be martyred, had joined them.

Then John said Jesus broke the sixth seal and there was a great earthquake (massive). The sun became as dark as black cloth and the moon became as red as blood. Then the stars of the sky fell to the earth like green figs falling from a tree that had been shaken by a strong wind. The sky was rolled up like a scroll and all the mountains and islands were moved from their places. "WOW", just in this paragraph, so much is happening. This is a tremendous mixture of upheaval. Look at the meteor that struck the earth in Winslow Arizona, that left a massive crater. They could be intercontinental ballistic missiles (ICBMs) that are shot from one point, and enter the atmosphere to come down again, hitting their target. Whatever it is, it's catastrophic." Whatever it is, you will know that it is the hand of God. Mountains and islands are going to disappear.

The Lord is going to shake this world to the point where the axis of the earth is going to shift. Just like God's Word says, every knee will bow and every tongue will confess that Jesus is Lord. We can bow our heads now and ask forgiveness of our sins, or hang on because it's only the beginning. It's going to get worse. When we get to the sixth vial that is poured out onto the earth, we see that it is parallel with the Sixth Seal being opened. They coincide with each other. With great earthquake islands being moved (probably another polar axis shift), this is called The Great Day of His Wrath. It's comforting that in 1 Thessalonians, God has not appointed us unto wrath. Paul also declares in Romans 5:9, That believers in Christ will be counted worthy to escape all of these things and will stand before the Son of Man.

In Chapter 7,of Revelation The four angels at the four corners of the earth will cause the rain to cease, and (Chapter 11) God sends his two witnesses, and they cause it not to rain for three and a half years. Here the rain was ceased, because the ocean waters evaporate into the atmosphere, and are then carried by the winds over the Earth. The winds are held back until the one hundred forty-four thousand are sealed, 12,000 from each tribe of Israel: Judah, Reuben, Gad, Asher, Naphtali, Manasseh, Simeon, Levi, Issachar, Zebulun, Joseph, Benjamin.

After this I saw a vast crowd, too many to count, from every nation and tribe and people and language, standing in front of the throne and before the Lamb. They were clothed in white robes and held palm branches in their hands and they were shouting with a great roar "salvation comes from our God who sits on the throne, and from the Lamb." All the angels were standing around the throne, and around the elders and the four living beings, and they fell before the throne with their faces to the ground and worship God. They sang, *Amen! blessing and glory and wisdom and thanksgiving and honor and power and strength belong to our God forever and ever, Amen.* Then one of the 24 elders asked me who are these who are clothed in white where did they come from? And I said to him sir you are the one who knows. Then he said to me, these are the ones who died in the Great Tribulation. They have washed their robes in the blood of the Lamb and made them white, we remember when Jesus made his descent from the Mount of Olives on the road to Bethany the crowd, we're waving palm branches and the multitude were saying Hosanna, Hosanna, blessed is he who comes in the name of the Lord. So here is the crowd now in heaven, a great number of them from all over the world, from all the various races and ethnic groups. They're the same salvation to our God which sits upon the throne and unto the Lamb" And all of these angels stood about the throne and about the elders and four living creatures and they fell before the throne on their faces and worshiped God, saying, Blessings and glory and wisdom and thanksgiving and honor and power and might be unto our God forever and ever amen.

Remember, the parable Jesus gave to the kingdom of heaven was likened to the man going through the field, which is the world discovering a treasure who for the joy, went out and sold everything so that he could buy the field and have the treasure. Jesus gave his life to purchase the world in order that he might purchase the treasure. So, if you only knew, Paul said, how the Lord treasures and values you. Peter wrote that we are His peculiar treasure. God treasures us, and we are His inheritance as we proceed into the judgments of God that are going to come upon the earth.

The fresh water supply is going to be polluted. When God sent his two witnesses, they stopped it from raining for at least three and a half years. Imagine no rain. There will be tremendous drought and famine. The crops will fail. God is going to give power to the Sun to scorch mankind. The hottest temperature I've been in was 118 degrees, and it was unbearable. The Lord ends this chapter for the Lamb, which, in the midst of the throne shall feed them, and shall lead them unto the living fountains of waters, and God shall wipe away all tears from their eyes.

We come back to the seven seals, the title deed to the earth that Jesus is opening to prove His right to redeem. Before we move on, and as things begin to open up, within the last 2 weeks a police officer killed an African-American man needlessly. It was caught on TV in Minnesota. This event sent the U.S. and the world into chaos, as some of the protests were peaceful. On the other side, there has been total anarchy in the streets - setting police cars on fire, looting, setting buildings on fire. Where is everything heading, Lord, with this destruction in the major cities? We need to say, *Thy Kingdom come Thy Will be done on earth as it is in heaven.*

Let's look at II Peter 3:9(NKJ) which says that The Lord is not slack concerning His promise, as some count slackness, but He is long-suffering towards us - not willing that any should perish but that all should come to repentance. "It's coming." Luke 21:25(NkJ) says And there will be signs in the sun, in the moon and the stars, and on earth. There will be distress of nations with perplexity, and waves roaring men's hearts - failing them with fear and the expectation of those things which are coming to the earth.

Chapter 12

So here we are! Jesus has opened the seventh Seal. There was silence, and John said that this silence lasted for about half an hour. There was all of this activity, then complete silence. Then here comes the seven trumpet judgments. I'm sure all of us have seen firework displays on the 4th of July. First, you see the primary explosion, then inside that primary explosion is another explosion. That's how it's going to be at the end of the seventh seal.

Seven angels were standing before God and were given the seven trumpets. There are cherubim angels around the Throne of God, and there are archangels, the Bible speaks of two, Michael and Gabriel. Another angel came with the golden censer, which was for the prayers of the saints upon the golden altar before the Throne of God. This angel was believed to be Jesus Christ, and we can see him work as a mediator and our great High Priest. Remember the tabernacle that was set upon the earth was an exact replica of heaven, and the priest would go in and offer the Lord sacrifices for the people. The incense would rise before the altar, which was called The Mercy Seat and was outside the Holy of Holies. So again, the prayers of the saints are being offered unto God the Father. *How long, O Lord, before you avenge our blood against those on earth who had slain them.*

We can see that God's judgments are coming. The angel then took the censer, which was filled with fire, and threw it to earth, and there were noises - thunder and lightning and an earthquake. The first angel sounded, and hail and fire followed, mingled with blood, and they were thrown to the earth. One third of the trees burned up and all grass was burned. The second trumpet sounded, and something like a great mountain burning with fire was thrown into the sea, and a third of the sea became blood and a third of the living creatures in the sea died, and a third of the ships were destroyed. There is concern in our solar system of an asteroid belt. There is concern by scientists and astronomers.

Outside of Tucson, Arizona on Kit Mountain, there is a telescope, and their job there is plotting and searching for asteroids that present a real threat to the earth. There are some 2000 asteroids that have been identified, and their orbit can ultimately bring them into a collision course with the earth. There are another 2,000 that could hit the earth. If an asteroid measuring 1km impacted the earth, it would do more damage than all-out nuclear warfare. The only thing that it would not leave is the effects of radiation. The asteroid that hit outside of Winslow, Arizona was 3 miles in diameter and 522 feet deep. If an asteroid hit from just the right direction, it could yank the earth off of its axis.

Scientists believe that in 1906, there was a great catastrophe in Siberia which flattened huge trees, laying them over like toothpicks for several hundred miles. This is a threat and a concern. Remember, Jesus said that the stars of heaven are going to fall like a fig tree casting forth its untimely fruit. We can't forget the ICBM will be falling from the skies. The meteor showers we see here are nothing compared to what is going to happen as we move forward.

The earth, at this point, has been under severe drought. The grass and trees will be dried up. The second angel sounded and there was a great mountain burning with fire, falling into the sea. Then, a gigantic asteroid or meteor falls into the sea, and the third part of the sea becomes blood, a result of the explosion of this massive object and disintegration killing off the fish. The ships probably could be destroyed by tidal waves and tsunamis. The third angel sounded, and there fell a great star from heaven, burning as if it were a lamp, and falling upon the third part of the rivers and on the fountains of waters. The name of the star is Wormwood. One third of the fresh water supply became wormwood poisonous and many men died. The fourth angel sounded and one third of the sun was smitten, one third of the moon, and a third of the stars.

If any of you have ever been in an area of California when there were fires, there would be tremendous burning to the point where the smoke actually blocked the light of the sun. There is no indication of what this might be. It could be a meteor shower, when they enter the earth's atmosphere and disintegrate. It could be fallout from nuclear weapons. When Mount Saint Helens erupted, I guess many years ago now, it blocked out the sun at mid-day. However, the Lord is going to do it. When He says it's going happen, it's going to be done. *And I beheld an angel flying through the midst of heaven saying with a loud voice, "Woe, Woe, Woe", to the inhabitants of the earth, by reason of the other voices of the trumpet, of the three angels which are yet to sound.*

Even in judgment, God's love still reaches out to mankind warning them. Remember this angel is orbiting the earth, and four angels have sounded, and there has been massive catastrophic devastation. What is to come will be even worse.

Chapter 13

We know that the world at this time is full blown into the occult and Satan worship. In the last paragraph of Luke 21, it says that they did not repent of their murders and their sorceries (witchcraft) or their sexual immorality or their thefts. There was total anarchy - so the Lord's going to give them what they want.

The fifth angel sounded and John said, *I saw a star falling from heaven to the earth.* To him was given a key to the bottomless pit. He opened the bottomless pit and we see the star that fell from heaven, and then the term him, and so this has to be Satan. This is the abyss (the abusso in Greek), which translates to bottom less pit, and it's probably right in the center of the earth. You know that hades was in the heart of the earth because right in the center of the earth you would be constantly falling, since the earth is continually rotating. You would be a constant state of falling in the bottomless pit, and this is where God incarcerates these demons.

When Jesus went to the region of Gerasenes, there was a man living among the tombs who was filled with many demons. When Jesus asked him his name he replied Legion, because of the many demons that took residence within this man. The demons said to Jesus, don't send us to the abusso before our time. There was a herd of swine nearby, and Jesus gave them permission to enter the swine. They did so, and the swine ran down the slope and into the water and drowned.

When Satan opened the bottomless pit there a rose great smoke, like the smoke from a great furnace, and the sun and the air were darkened. These demons came out as a swarm of locusts, and to them was given power. Just like the scorpions that were commanded not to harm the vegetation, they could not harm those who are sealed by God - and you know that those sealed by God are those who accepted Christ as their Savior and are sealed by the Holy Spirit. The shapes of the locusts were more like horses that were prepared for battle; and their heads were as it were crowns of gold. In both cases, were as the faces of men, and they had hair of women and their teeth were as the teeth of lions, and they had breast plates of iron, and the sound of their wings was as the sound of the horses with many chariots running into battle.

What is John really saying? Speculation says that this is a Blackhawk helicopter that had the face of a man. Perhaps he saw the man flying the helicopter through the windshield of the cockpit, the woman's hair could be the blades of the helicopter, hanging downward, the teeth. The front of the helicopter could be the breastplate of iron.

Just sitting there, picture in your mind what John is seeing, the sound of their wings was like the sound of many horses running to battle. How would John describe the sound of the engine of the helicopter and jet bombers, and the tail end goes up like a scorpion. Who knows? He was doing a pretty good job don't you think? They had tails like unto scorpions and there are were stings in their tails, and they had power to hurt men for 5 months.

It said that they had a king over them - an angel from the bottomless pit - and his name in Hebrew was Abaddon and in Greek,

Apollyon the Destroyer, which is Satan himself. In these last days God is going to release some bad dudes. These demons have been locked up. God is going to take death away. People will be trying to commit suicide and won't die. There will be some grotesque things happening. One has now passed but there are two more to come.

Now it says, *the sixth angel sounded and I heard a voice from the four horns of the golden altar which is before God, saying to the sixth angel which had the trumpet, loose the four angels which are bound in the great river Euphrates.* So, four angels were loosed, and these four had been bound for thousands of years, and were prepared for an hour and a day and a month and a year for to slay the third part of man left on the earth. These angels (demons) are so fierce that God kept them bound. Some of these things we covered briefly, but like anything in God's Word we can never read it enough.

The number of the army was 200 million. In 1965 China proclaimed they could man and army of this exact number. We can see in chapter 16 that the sixth angel poured out his bowl on the great river Euphrates, and it dried up so that the kings of the east could march their armies towards the west without hindrance. All the judgments of God are a result of the deplorable state that man is in. Man's heart is so hardened against God that they will not repent and turn toward the Lord. They continue to worship demons and idols made of gold silver, bronze, stone and wood. Idols can neither see nor hear nor walk. They did not repent of their murders or witchcraft, or their sexual immorality or their thefts.

John is giving us a little insight into future events the coming of Jesus Christ to the earth, to claim that which he purchased. Jesus paid the price for our redemption. John sees Jesus coming to the earth. His face shone and his feet were like pillars of fire, just like John described Jesus in chapter 1. In His hand was a small scroll (the title deed to the earth). His right foot was on the sea and his left foot on the land, and he gave a great shout like the roar of a lion, and when He shouted the seven thunders answered.

We have some Old Testament references. Jeremiah 25:31(Living Bible) says, the Lord will roar against his own land from his Holy dwelling in heaven. He will shout like those who tread grapes. He will shout against everyone on earth. Hosea 11:10(Living Bible) says, for someday the people will follow me. I the Lord will roar like a lion. In Joel, the Lord's voice will roar from Zion and thunder from Jerusalem. So, we and all creation will groan together, waiting and travailing for the glorious day when the Lord will come and claim that which he purchased. James says, establish yourselves, for the Lord is waiting for the perfect or complete fruit of harvest.

Peter said that the delay of the Lord would cause some people to scoff, *and in the last days scoffers will come saying, where is the promise of his coming since our fathers have fallen asleep all things continue as they were from the beginning.* 2 Peter 3:4 says, but Peter said God is not slack concerning his promises as some count slackness, but a day is as a thousand years to the Lord and a thousand years is as a day, and know that this delay is for redemption purposes, that more people might come in and be a part of the body of Christ. 2nd Peter 3:9. When God wishes to establish an oath - a promise - he can't swear by any higher so he swears by Himself. God intended that man would come to the knowledge of Him through nature. *When the seven thunders spoke, I was about to write but I heard a voice from heaven saying, keep secret what the seven thunders said and do not write it down. The voice which I heard from Heaven spoke unto me again to go and take the open scroll from the hand of the Angel who is standing on the sea and on the land. So, I went to the angel and told him to give me the small scroll. "Yes, take it and eat it, he said. It will be sweet as honey in your mouth but it will turn sour in your stomach. Then I was told you must prophesy again about many peoples, nations, languages and kings.* The idea is to devour the book and the contents therein.

Chapter 11. *Then I was given a measuring stick and I was told go and measure the temple of God and the alter, and count the number of worshippers. But do not measure the outer courtyard for it has been turned over to the nations.* Here he's talking about the Temple Mount, as this is where the temple is going to be built. This is where the Dome of the Rock Mosque currently exists - the Muslim shrine. But there is enough room to build the Jewish temple, and that's why it says don't measure the outside court, because it belongs to the gentiles.

This is Jesus speaking in verse 3: and I will give power to my two witnesses and they will be clothed in burlap (mourning). I will prophesy during 1,260 days (three and a half years). These two prophets are the two olive trees and the two lamp stands that God is sending. There are two witnesses to the Jewish people. God is going to deal with Israel.

In Malachi 4:1(LivingBible) The Lord of Heaven's armies says the day of judgment is coming, burning like a furnace. On that day, the arrogant and the wicked will be burned up like straw. They will be consumed – roots, branches and all.

One witness is Elijah, in the last book of the Old Testament. Malachi 4:5 (Living Bible)says, *look, I am sending you the Prophet Elijah before the great and dreadful day of the Lord arrives. His preaching will turn the hearts of fathers to their children and the hearts of the children to the father's. Otherwise, I will come and strike the land with a curse.* There is no doubt that Elijah is one of the witnesses, by the fact that these two witnesses called down fire from heaven.

The king sent out a captain with 50 men to arrest Elijah. The captain came and said to him, thou man of God come down, I have to arrest you. Elijah responded, if I am a man of God then let fire come down from heaven and consume you and your fifty men, and fire came down from heaven and consumed them. The king sent out another captain and fifty men, with the same result. So, you king, sent another captain with fifty men, but the captain approached Elijah with extreme caution, pleading with Elijah. He said sir, I am a married man have a wife and children and they love me. Have mercy on me. I'm following orders. I wish you would come with me please, the king would like to see you, and Elijah went with him. When Elijah was on earth he prayed, and it didn't rain for 3 and 1/2 years. He's going to duplicate this while these two witnesses are on the earth for three and a half years.

Also, it was with Elijah and Moses that Jesus took Peter, James, and this same John, up to the Mount of Transfiguration. Matthew 17:2(NKJ) says, Jesus led them up this high mountain where he transfigured himself before them. His face shone like the sun and his clothes became white as light, and behold Moses and Elijah appeared to them talking with Him. Verse 5 says that while Peter was still speaking, behold a bright cloud overshadowed them, and suddenly a voice came out of the cloud saying, *this is My Beloved Son, in whom I am well pleased. Hear Him!*

It says in Revelation 11:6,(NKJ) that these men have power to shut heaven so that no rain falls in the days of their prophecy, and they have power over waters to turn them to blood. This is one of the plagues Moses performed when God chose him to lead the Israelites out of bondage. They have the power to strike the earth with these plagues as often as they want. Enoch is another name for the other prophet. But Moses and Elijah seem to be the ones who will be witnesses for the Jewish people. Moses represents the Law and Elijah represents the Prophets.

Now when they have finished their testimony. They have an allotted time 1,260 days 3 and 1/2 years. The Beast that ascends from the Abyss, which is the bottomless pit, is the Antichrist, who shall make war against them and shall overcome them and kill them. He can do nothing until they have finished their testimony. This is the same for all of us. Our time here on earth will not be over until God is done with us. It says their dead bodies shall lie in the streets of the great City (Jerusalem), which is spiritually called Sodom and Egypt - where our Lord was crucified. Their bodies will lie in the street and they will not bury them for three and a half days. Those who dwell on the earth will rejoice over them. It's going to be like Christmas. They're going to make merry and give gifts. It's going to be a real hullabaloo.

Remember, John is writing this and they didn't have satellite TV like we have today. These two men that caused all this havoc are dead. All the eyes of the world will be focused on these two bodies - a worldwide celebration. Then after three and a half days the Breath of God entered them and they stood to their feet. It says that great fear fell on those who saw them (you think?), and they heard a loud voice from Heaven saying to them *come up here*, and they ascended to heaven in a cloud, and their enemies saw them.

In the same hour there was a great earthquake. Remember, when Jesus was crucified, there was a great earthquake, and a tenth part of the city fell. Seven thousand people were killed, and the rest were afraid and gave glory to the God of Heaven. The second woe has past, and behold, the third woe is coming quickly. Then the seventh angel sounded and there were great voices in heaven. The kingdoms of this world become the kingdoms of our Lord God and of his Christ, and He shall reign forever and ever. The judgments are coming in order to prepare earth for the return of Jesus Christ in the establishment of his kingdom.

The four and twenty elders who sat before God, fell upon their faces and worshiped God. And they said, *we give thanks to you Lord*

God, the almighty, the one who is and who always was, for now you have assumed your great power and have begun your reign. The nations were filled with wrath but now the time of your wrath has come. It's time to judge the dead and reward your servants, the prophets, as well as your holy people and all who fear your name: from the least to the greatest. It's time to destroy all who have caused destruction on the earth.

Then the temple of God was opened in Heaven and the Ark of the Covenant was seen in his temple, and there were lightning noises, thundering, an earthquake and great hail. Chapter 12 says, that there appeared a great wonder in heaven, a woman clothed with the sun and the moon under her feet and on her head, a crown of twelve stars. The identity of the woman is found in Genesis, as we read of the dream of Joseph, and how the sun and the moon and the 11 stars bowed down to him. The woman is the nation of Israel, the 12 tribes of Jacob. She, being great with child, traveling in childbirth, was ready to give birth. God's purpose for the nation of Israel is that they were to bring his Son, the Messiah, into the world to go forth and change the nation, and Israel was the nation. That is why they are the chosen people. God chose them, but they rejected His Son. These 2 wonders - the woman and Israel, were ready to bring forth the Messiah, and Satan was ready to destroy him as soon as he was born.

We can see in Matthew 2 that Herod had a private meeting with the wise men from the east. They were following the star that was leading them to Jesus. Herod was a paranoid person, and he stood about 4 feet and 11 inches tall. He was known as Herod the Great. He was consumed with building huge things such as temples, gardens, and forts. He killed his wife and sons and he felt that people were plotting to take his throne, so when he heard a king had been born, he felt threatened. He told the wise men to come back and tell him. He intended to kill the child, and when the wise men didn't come back, he ordered all children 2 years and under to be killed.

The Lord told Joseph to take the child and mother to Egypt until Herod's death. The dragon was ready to devour the child as soon as he was born. It says that the angels have rankings, and there were three high-ranking angels - Archangels Gabriel, Michael and Lucifer (Satan). When Lucifer rebelled against God, one-third of the Angels were involved with him. His tail drew a third of the stars of Heaven, and through them to earth. Verse 6. Then the woman Israel fled Into the wilderness where she has a place prepared by God that they should feed her there, 1,260 days (three and a half years). It is said that this place God prepared is The Rock City of Petra in Jordan. In Ezekiel 28:15,(Living Bible) God's Word says of Lucifer (Satan), *You are blameless in all you did from the day you were created until the day evil was found in you.* Verse 6 - *You were rich, but commerce led you to violence and you sinned, so I banished you in disgrace from the Mountain of God. I expelled you, oh mighty guardian, from your place among the stones of fire.* Verse 17 - *Your heart was filled with pride because of your beauty, and your wisdom was corrupted by your love of splendor. So, I threw you to the ground and exposed you to the curious gaze of kings.*

Verse 9 - When he realized that he had been thrown down to the earth, he pursued the woman (Israel) who had given birth to the male child. This reference is to Jesus, but she was given two wings like those of a great eagle. Could this reference be to an aircraft which was also known in the US as an eagle? She could fly to the place prepared for her in the wilderness, Rock City of Petra, free to escape to the mountains. Remember what we saw in Matthew 24 and Mark 13:14

So, you see what Jesus said regarding the abomination of desolation spoken of by Daniel the Prophet, when the Antichrist goes into the temple and proclaims that he is God. Then let those who are in Judea flee to the mountains let him who is on the housetop not go down into the house, and let him who is in the field not go back to get his clothes. For there will be greater anguish in those days than at any time since God created the world and it will never be so great again. In fact, unless the Lord shortens that time of calamity not a single person will survive – but for the sake of his chosen ones, he has shortened those days.

Ezekiel 38:16(Living Bible) You will attack My people, Israel, covering their land like a cloud. At that time in the distant future, I will bring you against my land as everyone watches (satellite T.V.) and my holiness will be displayed by what happens to you Gog (Russia). Then all the nations will know that I am the Lord.

Back track to Revelation 12:15(Living **Bible**). Then the Dragon (Satan) tried to drown the woman (Israel) in a flood of water that flowed from his mouth. This flood is an army, but the earth helped her (Israel) by opening its mouth and swallowing the river that gushed from the mouth of the Dragon. It looks like God is going to open up the earth and swallow the army. The Dragon (Satan) was angry at the woman (Israel) and declared war against the rest of her children, all those who kept God's Commandments and maintained their testimony for Jesus, those who accepted Christ as their Savior (at this time born–again believers). Then the dragon (Satan) took his stand on the shore.

Chapter 13 (Living Bible)I saw the Beast (Antichrist) rising up out of the sea. The sea represents the multitude of people, having seven heads and ten horns. The seven heads, all seven mountains, is believed to be Rome surrounded by seven hills. The ten horns are 10 kings, a ten-nation confederation out of the E. U. It's believed that the Antichrist and false prophet are going to rise from the European Union. Many Bible scholars believe that these two are alive somewhere today. Daniel described this Beast. The Lord told Daniel that these Ten kings were going to give their powers to the Beast. Now the Beast which I saw was like a leopard, his feet of a bear, and his mouth like the mouth of a lion. The dragon (Satan) gave him his power, his throne, and great authority. The Antichrist will have the characteristics of these world powers. Daniel 7 also talks about the Antichrist. In Verse 8 it says, As I was looking at the horn and suddenly another small horn (Antichrist) appeared among them. This little horn had eyes like human eyes and a mouth that was boasting arrogantly. Three out of the ten-nation confederacy are not going along with him. He violently attacks them because there aren't joining in with the Antichrist. I continue to watch because I could hear the little horns' boastful speech.

We also see in Verse 2 - In my vision, that night I, Daniel, saw a great storm churning the surface of a great sea. We see in Revelations 13:1 that she saw the Beast rising up out of the sea, the Antichrist rising out of the sea of humanity. Verse 13 - As my vision continued that night, I saw someone like a son of man coming with the Clouds of Heaven. He was given authority, honor and sovereignty over all the nations of the world, so that people of every race nation and language would obey him.

Daniel 7:15(Living Bible) and 16 v.15 - I Daniel was troubled by all I had seen and my vision terrified me. Verse 16 (Living Bible) So I approached one of those standing beside the throne and asked him what it meant. He explained it to me. These four huge beasts represent four kingdoms that will arise from the earth. In the end, the holy people of the Most-High will be given the kingdom and they will rule forever and ever.

Verse 19 (Living Bible)Then I wanted to know the true meaning of the fourth Beast, the one so different from the others and so terrifying. It had devoured and crushed its victims with iron teeth and bronze claws, trampling their remains beneath its feet. This horn seemed greater than the others, and it had human eyes and a mouth that was boasting arrogantly.

Verse 23 - Then he said to me, this fourth world power that will rule the Earth will be different from the others. It will devour the entire world, trampling and crushing everything in its path. Then another king will arise - different from the other ten - who will subdue three of them. He will defile the most-high. He will try to change their sacred festivals and laws and they will be placed under his control for three and a half years. It says for time - 1 year times 2 years and a half a time (half a year).

Daniel 11:36 (NKJ) Then the king (Antichrist) shall do according to his own will: He will exalt and magnify himself above every god. He shall speak blasphemies against the God of gods, and shall prosper till the wrath has been accomplished, for what has been determined shall be done. He shall do as he pleases, considering himself to be under no authority, setting himself above any and every god, speaking blasphemies in the morning worship until the end of the tribulation.

The Antichrist will worship gold and silver as he defeats these countries. He gathers their wealth to fund his army. He shall enter these countries and overwhelm them as he passes through. He shall enter the glorious land (Israel) and many countries shall be overthrown. These verses announce the arrival of the end of the tribulation.

The Antichrist's victory and power will increase until he has control of the wealth of these nations, yet his global empire will slowly begin to disintegrate with the word coming out of the East, and the forces from the North that challenge his claim to global domination. This will be one battle in a series of major skirmishes across the earth, and they will culminate in the forces of Satan being under the direction of the Antichrist. We see that Satan is right in the middle of everything that is going on. These armies are coming from the East and the North, all of them marching to destruction at the battle of Armageddon.

Let's head back to Revelation 13. The dragon (Satan) gave him his power, his throne, and great authority. Then there is an assassination attempt against the Antichrist, a mortal head wound, it says. His deadly wound was healed. Remember that Satan cannot create - he can only duplicate - and he certainly cannot resurrect anyone from the dead. It's going to look like the Antichrist died and miraculously lived: and all the world marveled and followed the Beast.

So, they worshiped the dragon (Satan), and this is what Satan wants. He gave his authority to the Beast and they worshiped the Beast, saying "who is like the beast? Who is able to make war with him?" What we have at this point is full blown satanism and Satan worship. He was given a mouth of speaking great things and blasphemies, and he was given authority to continue for 42 months. Then he opened his mouth in blasphemy against God, to blaspheme his name, his Tabernacle, and those who dwell in Heaven. It was granted to him to make war with the saints. These are believers who have given their lives to Christ through the witness of the hundred forty-four thousand and the testimony of the two witnesses. Authority was given him over every tribe, tongue and nation. The earth will worship him whose names have not been written in the Book of Life, of the Lamb slain from the foundation of the world. Their fate is sealed and they are doomed.

Then I saw another Beast coming out of the earth. This is the false prophet, and he had two horns like a lamb and spoke like a dragon. He is the Imposter. He is pretending to be like Jesus but he's full of Satan - evil through and through. He exercises all of the authority of the first beast and causes the earth and those who dwell upon it to worship the first beast, whose deadly wound was healed. The result of the assassination attempt is going to leave the Antichrist maimed.

Zechariah 11:17(NKJ) - Woe to the worthless shepherd who leaves the flock! A sword shall be against his arm and his right eye. His arm shall completely wither and his right eye shall be totally blinded. In Matthew 7:15(NKJ) Jesus said to beware of false prophets who come in sheep's clothing but inwardly they are ravenous wolves. You may say to yourself, as I do, who could out-and-out worship Satan?

In 1966 Anton Levey founded the Church of Satan and eventually wrote the Satanic Bible. He set the teachings and rituals of this church. Satanism is large right now. It's a dark underground society, until you talk to the police departments across this nation and world, where they've come across areas in which Satanic rituals have been performed. This occult is widespread, but at this time it is the form of worship that this false prophet causes the world, small and great, rich and poor, to worship. The Antichrist will be able to call fire to come down from heaven. Satan is orchestrating everything, but remember he can only duplicate. As with the two witnesses in chapter 11,they brought fire from heaven.

Now these two in Chapter 13 of Revelation duplicate the same thing, and they are also going to create an image of the Antichrist. It will probably be set up in the Jewish temple, where the Antichrist helped the Jews rebuild their temple at the beginning of the first three and half years. In the middle of the last seven years the Antichrist will enter the temple, claiming to be worshipped as God. This is the abomination of the desolation. It says that they make this image come to life.

John is writing this in the first century and, of course, he did not have computer technology. This can easily be done in the world we live in today, but to those living in the world today, it's going to be some phenomenal thing. We have to remember that Satan is The Great Deceiver, as Jesus describes him.

They are going to set up a one world government, and you will have to take this Mark on your forehead or on your hand. John is specific here that you won't be able to buy or sell without this mark, and the specific number 666. If anyone takes this mark, they are done - their fate is sealed. If anybody takes his mark, don't do it, bend your knee to Christ. Give your life to Jesus. Repent of your sins, and you're going to have to die as a martyr, but hang on you'll make it. Look to the Lord for your strength, hang on and don't give in. It's going to be hard because of what Satan said to God in Job 2:4.(Living Bible) Satan replied to the Lord "skin for skin." A man will give up everything he has to save his life. Kids in school today are being taught about globalism and world order. The purpose of this is for the operation or planning of economic and foreign policy on a global basis. World order: a system controlling events in the world, especially a set of arrangements to establish international preservation for global political stability.

Chapter 14 - We are halfway through the tribulation at this point. In chapter 11 we had God's two witnesses. Their three-and-a-half-year reign is through the Antichrist, who made war against them. He killed the two witnesses and their bodies lay in the streets of Jerusalem. God then resurrected them, and they ascended to Heaven. Now we have the 144,000; Billy Graham's witnessing for the Lord; then God's Air Force; angels warning the people of earth, proclaiming the eternal good news; and God's Word to every nation tribe language and people. Fear God! He shouted his glory to him, for the time has come when he will sit as judge. People on the earth are completely involved in satanic and demonic worship, but God never gives up trying to save people from his judgments, that are still coming and intensifying. All the judgments that have come, have brought total devastation, but their hearts are hardened. Another angel followed him through the sky shouting, Babylon has fallen. This is one world government.

Then a third angel followed them shouting - anyone who worships the Beast and his statue, or who accepts his mark on the forehead or on the hand, must drink the wine of God's anger, as it has been poured full strength into God's cup of wrath. They will be tormented with fire and burning sulfur in the presence of the holy angels and the Lamb. The smoke of their torment will rise forever and ever, and they will have no relief, day or night, for they have worshiped the Beast and his statue and have accepted the mark of his name. This means that God's holy people must endure persecution patiently, obeying his commands and maintaining faith in Jesus.

Revelation chapter 14 Verse 13 - And I heard a voice from heaven saying write this down: blessed are those who die in the Lord's Spirit. They are blessed indeed, for they will rest from their hard work, for their good deeds follow them.

2nd Peter 3:9 \(Living Bible) The Lord isn't really being slow about his promise as some people think. No, he is being patient for your sake. He does not want anyone to be destroyed, but wants everyone to repent.

Luke 21:34(NKJ) But take heed to yourselves lest your hearts be weighed down with carousing, drunkenness, and the cares of this life, and that day come, and you, unexpectedly. So, it will come as a snare upon all those who dwell on the face of the earth. Watch, therefore, and pray always that you may be counted worthy to escape all these things that will come to pass, to stand before the Son of Man."

Matthew 13:24(NKJ) Another parable He put forth to them says, the kingdom of heaven is like a man who sowed good seed in his field, but while the man slept, his enemy came and sowed tares among the wheat and went his way. When the grain had sprouted and produced a crop, the tares also appeared. So, the servants of the owner came and said to him, sir, did you not sow good seed in your field? How then does it have tares? He said to them, an enemy has done this. The servant then asked him, do you want us then to go and gather them up? He said no, lest while you gather them you uproot the wheat with them. Let both grow together until the time of harvest, and at the time of harvest, I will say to the reapers, first gather together the tares and bind them in bundles to burn them, but gather the wheat into my barn.

Verse 36 - Jesus explains the parable of the tares. When his disciples came to him and asked him to explain the parable of the tares of the field, he told them that he who sows the good seed is the Son of Man and the field is the world. The good seed represents the sons of the kingdom but the tares are the sons of the wicked one, and the enemy that sowed them is the devil. The harvest is the end of the age and the reapers are the angels.

Therefore, as the tares are gathered and burned in the fire, so it will be at the End of the Age. The Son of Man will send out his angels and they will gather out of his kingdom all things that offend, and those who practice lawlessness and will cast him into the furnace of fire.

Revelation 14 Verse 14 (NKJ) Then I looked and behold a white cloud, and on the cloud set one like the Son of Man, having on his head a golden crown and in His hand a sharp sickle. This is Jesus – and judgment is coming. Then another angel came from the temple (which is in heaven) with a sharp sickle. What we have here is the judgment of the last battle of Armageddon in the valley of Megiddo.

We can look at Isaiah 63 (LivingBible) which says, Who is this who comes from Edom from the city of Bozrah with his clothing stained red? who is this in royal robe with his great strength? It is I the Lord announcing your salvation! It is I the Lord who has the power to save! why are your clothes so red as if you have been treading out grapes? I have been treading the winepress alone, as no one was there to help me. In my anger I have trampled my enemies as if you were grapes, in my fury I have trampled my foes. Their blood has stained my clothes, for the time has come for me to avenge my people, to ransom them from their oppressors. I was amazed to see that no one intervened to help the oppressed, so I myself stepped in to save them with my strong arm, and my wrath sustained me. I crushed the nations in my anger and made them stagger and fall to the ground, spilling their blood upon the earth. The great wine press was trampled outside the city, and the blood came out of the wine press and went up to the horse's bridle for one thousand six hundred furlongs. The blood will flow to a horse's bridle four feet deep, 180 miles long.

In Daniel 11, we see the armies of the north coming against the Antichrist, the revised Roman Empire, which is coming out of the West. It says that no one will be able to stop him, for warships from the western coastland will scare off this advancing army from the North. The Antichrist is on the move, and all of these armies are headed to Armageddon.

Verse 44 - Then there is news from the East, and here comes a massive Army of 200 million. The kings of the East and the North will alarm the Antichrist, and he will set out in great anger to destroy and obliterate many. He will stop between the glorious holy mountain and the sea, and will pitch his royal tents. While these armies amass, there will be two to three hundred million soldiers, and all the kings of the East will be two hundred million strong. Let's try and wrap our heads around this number. If one man had 20 square feet 5' in the front and 5' in the back and 5 feet on each side of him, the width of this massive army would stretch one and a half miles wide and the length would be one hundred and eighty miles. This is massive. Can you envision 180 miles from where you live? There will be devastation from these armies with their nuclear weapons. No wonder the Lord said that unless these days be shortened there wouldn't be anyone who would survive.

Revelation:Chapter 15 - Here we have a prelude to the final seven plagues, these last seven bowls after which God's judgments will be completed - and they will be bad. God is preparing the Earth for His Son's reign: and I saw as if it were a sea of glass mingled with fire. This is the sea of glass that is before the Throne of God for the fiery judgments that are coming.

There are those standing on the sea, and they are given the harps of God. They are the redeemed of Israel who have been saved during the Great Tribulation. So, they sing the song of Moses, the servant of God, and the song of the Lamb saying, great and marvelous are the works of Lord God Almighty, just and true are thy ways.

There will never be a question or a doubt of the righteousness of God when the final time comes. Throughout all eternity there can never be any challenge to the fullness of God. God could have created us as robots, but didn't. He gave us free will. Throughout the tribulation, God has reached out to man, that we can see his declaration. Holy and true are thy ways, thy judgments, O Lord. even with Jesus' death, God protected the innocent. Pilate said, I find no fault with Him. Judas said, I have betrayed innocent blood. The thief on the cross said to the other, we deserve to be here but this man has done nothing wrong. Who shall not fear thee, O Lord, and glorify thy name?

Afterward I looked and beheld the temple of the tabernacle of testimony, and heaven was opened. The seven angels came out of the temple, having the seven plagues, clothed in pure white linen and having their breasts girded with golden girdles. These angels must be of a higher ranking, as they are wearing priestly clothing. These angels are bringing the seven final plagues of the judgments of God. One of the four cherubim gave the seven angels seven vials (little vials full of the wrath of God). The dictionary meaning of a vial is a small container, as for medicine, made of glass or plastic. God is about to pour some harsh medicine on the Earth from these vials. God does not delight in the death of the wicked.

Ezekiel 33:11 - God says turn ye, turn ye, for why will you die? Behold I have no pleasure in the death of the wicked. So, God's final plagues are poured out, and God sits in the temple weeping over man's rebellion. We see in Matthew 23:37 that Jesus was looking at Jerusalem and he began to weep. O Jerusalem, Jerusalem, now that stoneth the prophets and all that have come from God to thee. I would have gathered you together as a hen gathers her chicks, but you would not let me. John 14:9(Living Bible) - Jesus said I and the Father are one, you see me, then you've seen the Father. Jesus said pray always that you will be counted worthy to escape these things that are going to come to pass upon the earth that you might be standing before the Son of Man.

The technology is here: computer chips, smart cards. You pull up or go to a restaurant, pull out your iPhone and pay your bill. So, to take a mark to buy or sell is here. This technology in an altered form already exists. The words of Jesus are telling us today, "Watch ye therefore and be ready, for you know not the day or the hour the Son of Man is coming.

Chapter 15 - The temple of God was filled with the smoke from the glory of God and is closed to man. The cherubim gave these angels vials of wrath to pour out onto the earth.

Revelation 16 I heard a loud voice from the temple saying to the seven angels: Go your ways, pour out the bowls of the Wrath of God upon the Earth. So, this command was given by God to these angels. He dispatched them with the Seven Final Plagues, with which He will smite the earth prior to the sending of His Son to take dominion and control and to rule the earth. The first angel poured out his vial upon the earth, and horrible malignant sores broke out on everyone who had the mark of the beast. These oozing, wet ulcer-like sores are on the people who follow the beast. The fate of these people is sealed. There is no hope. They have taken this mark in rebellion against God.

In Matthew it says that in the end the Lord is going to separate the sheep from the goats – believers from non-believers. These sores, possibly from radiation burns, do not heal. God is making a distinction here between those who are faithful to Him and those who are following the beast. God is now making a difference.

We can remember when God poured the plagues on the Egyptians with Moses. God protected the Israelites from those judgements. There was darkness over the land of Egypt, but there was light in the camp of Israel. God made provisions to protect His people. They put blood on the lentils and the door posts of the Israelis, and the angel of death passed over their houses and struck the first born of the Egyptians. God was making the difference between those who were His and those who were not.

The second angel poured out his bowl upon the sea, and it became like the blood of a corpse, and everything in the sea died. The third angel poured his bowl upon the fresh water and springs, and they became blood.

Then John heard the angel over the waters say:

> *You are Just, O Holy One, who is and who always was*
> *Because you have sent these judgments,*
> *Since they shed the blood*
> *Of your holy people and your prophets*
> *You have given them blood to drink.*
> *It is their just reward*
> *And I heard a voice from the altar saying,*
> *Yes, O Lord God the Almighty,*
> *Your judgments are true and just.*

God sent this same plague to Pharoah and the Egyptians through Moses. How that happened is speculation, but it will happen just the way God said it will happen.

The fourth angel poured out his bowl upon the sun, causing it to scorch everyone with fire. Everyone was burned by this blast of heat, and they cursed the name of God who had control over all these plagues. They did not repent of their sins and turn to God, so God's judgments fell. The sun is now scorching men. How this will be accomplished is speculation. We know according to God's Word that the sun will be darkened before the day the Lord comes and the moon will turn to blood. We know something about stars and we know that the sun is a star, and that before a star dies it gets super bright and extremely hot. It's called a Super Nova.

We know that the ozone layer is being affected by the fluorocarbon gases that come from pressurized cans of shaving cream, hairspray, deodorants, etc., and we know of all the nuclear weapons going off around the world. So, the ozone layer is gone and the sun is scorching everyone on earth. I cannot imagine. The hottest temperature I've experienced is around 118-120 degrees, and it was unbearable. The ozone layer is a protective blanket. Maybe this is a nuclear holocaust. If a person is exposed to ultra-violet rays, it creates burns, oozing sores and skin cancer. You know that it's going to be bad by the words of the Bible - everyone burning with its fire. Everyone was burned by the blast of heat.

Then the fifth angel poured out his bowl upon the throne of the beast, and his kingdom was plunged into darkness. His subjects ground their teeth in anguish. God put this plague of darkness on Pharoah and the Egyptians. So, the Lord is giving the Antichrist and his kingdom this plague, so much so that they ground their teeth and - this is how stupid they are – they cursed the Lord God for their pain and sores. This is how much they are into Satan-worship; it says they did not repent of their evil deeds and turn to God.

Then the sixth angel poured out his bowl upon the great Euphrates River, and it dried up, so that the Kings from the East could march their armies toward the West without hindrance.

This is from the trumpet.com, June 11, 2014. The Ataturk Dam in Turkey dries up the Euphrates. This 1700-mile river, in an impending water shortage, threatens millions in the Middle East. The Syrian civil war has, once more, taken a dire turn for the worse. Turkey has altered its strategy against its opponents, the forces of Syrian President Bashar Assad. Instead of simply aiding the Syrian rebels, Turkey is now also killing them with dehydration. The problem is that this brutal act threatens the lives of millions of Syrian and Iraqi citizens.

The crisis revolves around the Euphrates River, which quickly became the Euphrates Creek after Turkey completely cut off the water flow upstream of Syria, reported Al Akhbar on May 30th. The Euphrates originates in Turkey and passes through the Ataturk Dam. They can actually dry up the Euphrates River. So, God is going to gather together the nations into the area of Israel, from the Valley of Megiddo to Edom. So, God now dries up the Euphrates to prepare the way for the Kings of the East - China and all of her vast hordes of people in India, Pakistan, Japan, moving in from the East.

And I saw three unclean spirits like frogs (demons) that came out of the mouth of the dragon, and out of the mouth of the beast, and out of the mouth of the false prophet. When Jesus cast out demons, they would come out screaming as they departed out of the mouth of Satan, the Antichrist and the false prophets. It even sounds creepy. These demons, working miracles, go forth unto the kings of the earth and the world. Together they go to the battle of the Great day of God Almighty. These demonic forces are going to gather these kings of the earth to Armageddon, where they will seek to make war against Jesus Christ at His return.

It is said that Hitler and his generals were in to what is known as white magic. These demonic forces were guiding him, and this explains those horrible atrocities. We know that Satan is controlling governments around the world today, and these nations are going to be sucked in by demonic forces.

They won't know why they are heading to the Valley of Megiddo for the last battle when Jesus returns. In Chapter 16 of Revelation (Living Bible) Verse 15, Jesus says "Look, I will come as unexpectedly as a thief. Blessed, are all who are watching for me, who keep their clothing ready so they will not have to walk around naked and ashamed."

Then the seventh angel poured out his bowl into the air, and a mighty shout came from the throne in the temple, saying - It is finished. Jesus said this from the cross. Now Jesus is saying it is finished because the wrath of God has been poured out thereover. Then the thunder crashed and rolled and lightning flashed, and a great earthquake struck. The worst since people were placed on earth. This earthquake will be felt worldwide. Then Jerusalem was split into three sections, and the cities of many nations fell into heaps of rubble. The earth is utterly shaken. Verse 19 mentions the cup of wine of the fierceness of His wrath.

Verse 20 - Then every land is fled away and the mountains were not found. What is causing the earth to convulse? It is all coming from the hand of the Lord. Could the earth possibly be hit by a giant asteroid that causes this polar axis shift? Who knows? Then it says great hail from heaven fell upon men. Each hailstone about the weight of a talent (100-125 pounds). It says that men blasphemed God because of the plague of hail, since that plague was exceedingly great. In the Old Testament, if you blasphemed the name of God the punishment was stoning. So, God is stoning mankind with these massive hailstones. Their hearts are still hardened – unbelievable.

Chapter 17 - God is going to judge the false religions. The Lord has judged Israel before, for their worship of Baal. Jeremiah 6 - During the reign of King Josiah, the Lord said to me, have you seen what fickle Israel has done? Like a wife who commits adultery, Israel has worshiped other gods on every hill and under every tree – all of these shrines to Baal. I thought, after she has done all this, she will return to me. But she did not return, nor her faithless Israel, because of her adultery. But that treacherous sister, Judah, had no fear, and now she, too, has left me and given herself to prostitution. This is how seriously God takes these false religions, calling them prostitutes and adulterers.

Hosea 1:2 - This will illustrate how Israel has acted like a prostitute by turning against the Lord and worshiping other gods. Deuteronomy 6:5 - You shall love the Lord your God with all of your heart, with all your soul, and with all your strength. We have to love him with every fiber of our being. He wants all of our love. Luke 16:13(Living Bible) - No one can serve two masters. For you will hate one and love the other. You will be devoted to one and despise the other. You cannot serve both God and money (the world).

Spiritually, this is a false religious system, leading men to follow the Antichrist. He is the scarlet beast. The woman is this false religion. Adultery is the worship of another god, other than Jesus Christ and their relationship with God. So, false worship of other gods is spiritual harlotry. Jesus told us in Matthew 7:15(Living Bible), so it is actually a warning – Beware of false prophets who will come looking like sheep but inwardly they are ravenous wolves. This chapter is what Jesus is talking about.

Babylon is used in the scriptures as a symbol of confusion. It was Babylon in rebellion against God that decided to build a tower, whereby they could communicate with the universe. Everyone at that time spoke the same language. Then God said, "Look what man is seeking to do now. If we don't stop him, he is going to be delving into areas where he has no business. So, God brought the confusion of tongues. This is where babble came from — the unintelligible sounds of these different languages. The people began to migrate away from that area and into their own groups. Babylon started these cultic practices. They worshiped Nimrod, who was a mighty hunter against the Lord, and his wife Symeramus, also known as Ashtart.

There are many stories involving Nimrod Semiramis and Tammuz, these characters being the start of pagan god worship throughout the known world. The most popular version is that Nimrod and Semiramis were King and Queen of Babylon. They ruled the people and turned them against God. However, in time Nimrod died. Semiramis, in a desperate attempt to hold onto her throne, devised a plan that would ultimately lead to not only retaining the throne, but elevating her to the status of goddess.

Semiramis claimed that after Nimrod died, he ascended to the sun and became the sun god himself. She then told the people that her son was the reincarnation of the sun god, and that she had been impregnated by the rays of the sun. She conceived a son and named him Tammuz. Tammuz, it said, was killed by a wild boar, and his body lay there for three days and then he resurrected.

The people celebrated his resurrection by coloring eggs and by worshipping the rabbit, known for its productivity. They had a great celebration that they called Ashtart, which is where we get our word, Easter. He was supposedly born on December 25th, and his birthday was celebrated by bringing trees into your home and decorating them with silver and gold and various decorations. The evergreen tree was the symbol of life. They would have parties, gift-giving and drunken orgies. We made Easter the celebration of Jesus's Resurrection, and Christmas his birthday.

These celebrations were of Babylonian origin. The Catholic religion adopted a lot of these pagan rituals, the worship of mother and child with a halo around them, rosary prayer beads, having a priest intercede for you and your sins. We see in the scriptures that this is totally false. The Bible tells us that there is one God, and one mediator between God and man – Christ Jesus.

Purgatory is a waiting place - a place or state of suffering - inhabited by the souls of sinners who are expiating their sins before going to Heaven. The Bible tells us, absent from the body present with the Lord. Hebrews 9:27 says that just as each person is destined to die once, and after that comes Judgement. There are many others, such as how they idolize one man, the Pope. I didn't say this – God says it.

Romans 3:23 - For everyone has sinned. We all fall short of God's glorious standards. Plus, it said that the wealth in the Catholic religion cannot be calculated. Including real estate, they have, gold, silver, money, and they have their own city – Vatican City. We can see this harlot, this false religion. This woman wore purple and scarlet clothing and beautiful jewelry made of gold and precious gems and pearls. The Vatican has adopted this scarlet color. The woman rode this scarlet beast, which is the Antichrist.

So, we see that the Antichrist is being led by a false religion on this woman's forehead. This mysterious name was written – Babylon, the Great Mother of all prostitutes and obscenities in the world.

Verse 9 calls for a mind with understanding. The seven heads of the beast represent the seven hills where the woman rules. We know that the Antichrist is going to rise out of the European Union, but he is ruling from Rome. When John wrote this, everybody knew the seven hills was Rome. It was like us saying The Big Apple - New York or the Windy City - Chicago. How about the city by the bay – San Francisco. I got this from Jon Courson. This is a great illustration, and I think all of us can grasp it. This is the revised Roman Empire, is the woman, the Catholic religion that the Antichrist and false prophets will use. The Catholic religion is a world-wide religion.

Revelations 17-V.10 - Five kings have already fallen. The sixth now reigns and the seventh is yet to come, but his reign will be brief. The beast that was and is not, is himself also the eighth and is of the seven, and is going to perdition. Five emperors, Caesars, have passed. One is the Caesar ruling at the time of Revelation, which was Domitian, who is the sixth, (something interesting) and the other is yet to come.

The Antichrist is the seventh and he will continue for a short time. He will be assassinated. It will seem that he comes back from the dead. The beast that was and is not, is himself also the eighth and is of the seven and is going to perdition. So, the beast that is also the eighth is coming back more vicious than what he was – and that's hard to believe. He is totally controlled by Satan. The people on earth will marvel at the beast – these must be the ones who have taken the mark. It says whose names are not written in the Book of Life from the foundation of the world, will be amazed at the reappearance of the beast who had died.

Nero was known as the beast for the things he did. He had to be demon possessed. He would wrap Christians in the hides of wild animals, light his private gardens with the bodies of Christians. Then the beast turns on the woman. Then he said to me, the water which you saw where the harlot sits are peoples, multitudes, nations and tongues, and the ten horns which you saw on the beast are the ten-nation confederacy. He will hate the harlot, make her desolate and naked, eat her flesh and burn her with fire – totally destroy this false religion. For God has put it into their hearts to fulfill His purpose, to be of one mind and give their kingdoms to the beast until the words of God are fulfilled.

They are of one mind and they will give their power and authority to the beast. These ten nations are all in total worship of the Antichrist. They will make war with the Lamb at Armageddon and the Lamb will overcome them, for He is the Lord of lords and King of Kings, and those who are with Him are called chosen and faithful.

Chapter 18 - At the end of chapter 17, the Antichrist and the king's ten nations turned against the woman, the harlot, the false religion, and devoured her Babylon. Now there is Babylon, the economic and commercial city - the main hub of commercial flourishing. Some say this city is Rome, but other scholars say this is rebuilt Babylon, which was partially rebuilt when Saddam Hussein was in power in Iraq.

He spent hundreds of millions of dollars, started to rebuild this ancient historical city and uncovering the ruins. He brought in experienced Japanese archaeologists. Hussein even built a big palace there using the ancient stones of this city. It is said that after the Antichrist rebuilds this city, its commercialism will be something of great wealth. We might say the timeline cannot fit. Well, look at cities like Dubai – how fast those skyscrapers went up – and the Antichrist will build it big and fast, as he and the false prophet move their power to this city. Isaiah 13:19(NKJ), And Babylon, the glory of kingdoms. The beauty of the Chaldean's pride will be as when God overthrew Sodom and Gomorrah. Verse 20, It will never be inhabited nor will it be settled from generation to generation.

> Nor will the Arabian pitch tents there
> Nor will the shepherd make their sheepfolds there
> But the wild beasts of the desert will lie there
> And their houses will be full of owls
> Ostriches will dwell there,
> And wild goats will go there to dance
> The hyenas will howl in their citadels
> And jackals in their pleasant places
> Her time is near to come,

And her days will not be prolonged:
Jeremiah 51:1(NKJ) Thus says the Lord:
Behold I will raise up against Babylon
Against those who dwell in LebKamai
A destroying wind.
And I will send winnowers to Babylon,
Who shall winnow her and empty her
Land for the day of doom.
They shall be against her all around
Against her let the archer bend his bow
And lift himself up against her in his armor.
Do not spare her young men
Utterly destroy all her army
Thus, the slain shall fall in the land
of the Chaldeans
And those thrust through in her streets
For Israel is not forsaken nor Judah
By his God the Lord of hosts
Though their land was filled with sin
Against the Holy One of Israel
Flee from the midst of Babylon
And everyone save his life!
Do not be cut off in her iniquity
For this is the time of the Lord's vengeance.
He shall recompense her
Babylon was a golden cup in the Lord's hand.
That made the earth drunk
The nations drank her wine
Therefore, the nations are deranged
Babylon has suddenly fallen
And been destroyed.

Revelations 18:1(NKJ) After these things I saw another angel coming down from heaven, hauling great authority, and the earth was illuminated with his glory. And he cried mightily with a loud voice saying Babylon the great is fallen, and has become a dwelling place of demons, a prison for every foul spirit, and a cage for unclean and hated bird! For all the nations have drunk of the wine of the wrath of her fornication. The kings of the earth have committed fornication with her, and the merchants of the earth have become rich through the abundance of her luxury. This black gold, oil, is rich in this area of the world. *For her sins have reached to heaven and God has remembered her iniquities.* Render to her just as she rendered to you, and repay her double according to her works in the cup which she has mixed. Mix double for her, and she will be utterly burned with fire, for strong is the Lord God who Judges her.

Verse 9 - The kings of the earth who committed fornication and lived luxuriously with her, will weep and lament for her when they see the smoke of her burning, standing at a distance for fear of her torment, saying "Alas, Alas, that great city Babylon, that mighty city!" For in one hour your judgement has come.

What did John see here? In one hour, this great city was gone. We know that God totally destroyed Sodom and Gomorrah with fire and brimstone. This is probably the result of a nuclear weapon. It says they stand at a distance, probably because of the radiation fallout – can't go near.

The merchants of the earth will weep and mourn over her, for no one buys their merchandise anymore. I like how Jon Courson describes this as a department store. The first floor, gold, silver, precious stones and pearls – the jewelry floor. The next floor, the clothing department - fine linen and purple, silk and scarlet. The next floor – fine furniture and kitchen utensils; citron wood, every kind of object; ivory – every kind of object of most precious wood, bronze, iron and marble. The next floor, perfume and cologne, and cinnamon and incense, fragrant oil, frankincense. Then comes the food court, fine food, wine and oil, fine flour and wheat. Cattle and sheep, fine steak houses. The next floor, fine automobiles – Ferrari, Lamborghini, Bentley, Rolls Royce; it says horses and chariots. The next floor, sexual immorality, it says, bodies and souls of men. This is Saks Fifth Avenue, Rodeo Drive, the rich.

Verse 14 - The fruit that your soul longed for has gone from you, and all the things which are rich and splendid have gone from you, and you shall find them no more at all. The merchants of these things who became rich by her will stand at a distance for fear of her torment, weeping and wailing and saying, "Alas, Alas, that great city that was clothed in fine linen, and purple and scarlet, and adorned with gold and precious stones and pearls!" For in one hour, such great riches came to nothing. Everything ruined and in mere rubble.

There is something that is interesting: Every shipmaster, all who travel by ship, and as many as trade on the sea, stood at a distance and cried out when they saw the smoke of her burning saying, what is like this great city. We've got to remember that this is speculation. It says shipmaster and all who travel by ship. We can see that Rome isn't by any sea - neither is Babylon. So, John put out a mind teaser – food for thought - which is an interesting concept that ships are on the sea. John threw this thought out there that possibly is the United States. In Babylon we're surrounded by many waters; it's an interesting thought. Verse 19 says, how terrible, how terrible, for that great city.

The ship owners became wealthy by transporting her great wealth on the seas. In a single moment, it is all gone. Verse 21 says, then a mighty angel picked up a boulder the size of a huge millstone and he threw it into the ocean and shouted: Just like this great city Babylon

Will be thrown down with violence
And will never be found again
The sound of harps, singers, flutes and
trumpets will never be heard in you again.

John said this gives us a mental picture: no more music, Hard Rock Café, Planet Hollywood. No craftsman and no trades. The sound of the mill will never be heard in you again. No more construction specialists in their trades. These huge skyscrapers will be gone, and will never rise again. The construction will be gone.

Verse 23 - The light of a lamp
Will never shine in you again.
We can picture in our minds, if you've ever
flown into a major city, the lights of the homes —
everything gone.
For your merchants were the greatest
In the world, were the greatest in the world
No more voices of brides and grooms
And you deceived the nations with your sorceries.
Verse 24 - In your streets flowed the blood of the
Prophets and of God's holy people
And the blood of people slaughtered all
Over the world.

Chapter 19:1 - Let's look at this, after these things, after God's judgment of the woman, this harlot, this false religion, and Babylon, the commercial and economic hub of the world.

Verse 2(Living Bible)- His judgments are true and just. He has punished the great prostitute who corrupted the earth with her immorality. He has avenged the murder of his servant. You know, as I did this study, I have realized even more that I deserve death, and what God has done for me through His Son.

Romans 5:8-9 - But God demonstrates His love toward us in that, while we were still sinners, Christ died for us. Much more than having been justified by His blood, we shall be saved by this blood. We shall be saved from wrath through Him. Gal. 2:20 (NKJ) I have been crucified with Christ. It is no longer I who live, but Christ lives in me, and the life which I now live in the flesh, I live by faith in the Son of God who loved me and gave Himself for me.

This statement by the Lord Jesus really says it all. Matthew 7:13- Enter by the narrow gate; for wide is the gate and broad is the way that leads to destruction, and there are many who go in by it. Because narrow is the gate and difficult is the way which leads to life, and there are few who find it.

> Verse 4 - Then the twenty-four and the four living beings fell down and worshiped God who was sitting on the throne.
> They cried out, "Amen!
> Praise the Lord!"
> All his servants
> All who fear him
> from the least to the greatest"

Then I heard again what sounded like the shout of a vast crowd or the roar of a mighty ocean of waves, or the crash of loud thunder.

We who are in heaven will say praise the Lord! For the Lord Our God the Almighty reigns. Let us behold and rejoice and let us give honor to him, for the time has come for the wedding feast of the Lamb, and his bride has prepared herself. She (believers) has been given the finest of pure white linen to wear. For the fine linen represents the good deeds of God's holy people.

Then John fell down to worship the angel but was rebuked by him. The angel told John, I am a servant of God just like you and your brothers and sisters who testify about their faith in Jesus, and worship only God. For the essence of prophecy is to give a clear witness for Jesus. Verse 11 - Then I saw heaven opened. There are only two times that heaven is opened, Chapter 4 at the Rapture of the church, and here at the second coming of our Lord. A white horse was standing there and its rider was named Faithful and True, for He judges fairly and wages a righteous war. His eyes were like flames of fire - this means judgment is coming, and on His head were many crowns. A name was written on Him that no one understood except Himself, and he wore a robe dipped in blood, and his title was the Word of God.

The armies of Heaven are us, the church, if you're a believer in Christ (born again). We're in this army, and we're dressed in fine linen, following Him, on white horses. From his mouth came a sharp sword, which is the Word of God, to strike down the nations.

Hebrews 4:12 (Living Bible)For the Word of God is alive and powerful. It is sharper than the sharpest two-edged sword, cutting between the soul and spirit. Between the joint and marrow, it exposes our innermost thoughts and desires. Nothing in all creation is hidden from God. Everything is naked and exposed before His eyes and He is the one to whom we are accountable. Here we go, following the Lord to Armageddon, His second coming destination in the Valley of Megiddo Jezreel Valley.

He will release the fierce wrath of God Almighty, like juice flowing from the winepress. On his robe at his thigh was written this title - King of Kings and Lord of Lords. Then I saw an angel standing in the sun shouting to the vultures flying high in the sky.

Come gather together for the great banquet of God has prepared, and eat the flesh of kings generals and strong warriors of horses and their riders and all humanity, both free and slave small and great. The Antichrist and these many nations fighting against each other there in the valley of Megiddo when they see Jesus and all of us just follow. We won't be fighting. Jesus has it all handled.

Let's pick up with Verse 19 - Then I saw the Beast. By now we know this is the Antichrist and the kings of the world and their armies - two to three hundred million men - gathered together to fight against the one sitting on the horse and his army. The Beast was captured, and with him the false prophet who did mighty miracles on behalf of the Beast, and deceived all who accepted the mark of the beast, and worshiped his statue. The Antichrist and the false prophet were thrown alive into the fiery lake of burning sulfur. Their entire army was killed by the sharp sword that came forth from the mouth of the one riding the white horse, and vultures gorged themselves on the dead bodies.

At the end of chapter 19, the Lord came back to earth. This is His second coming. He destroyed the Antichrist and the false prophet. They were thrown into the Lake of Fire Gehenna. The armies of the earth were wiped out by merely the Word of the Lord, the blood from the battle flowing a horse's bridle deep for 180 miles.

Matthew 24:21 Living Bible) For there will be greater anguish than at any time since the world began and it will never be so great again. Matthew 25 - but when the Son of Man comes in his glory and all the angels with him, then he will sit upon His glorious throne. All the nations will be gathered in his presence and he will separate the people as a Shepherd, the sheep from the goats. He will place the sheep at his right hand and the goats at his left.

Then the King will say to those on his right, come, as you are blessed by my Father, and inherit the Kingdom prepared for you from the creation of the world. Then the King will turn to those on the left and say away with you, cursed ones, into the eternal fire prepared for the devil and his demons. And they will go away into eternal punishment, but the righteous will go to eternal life.

Isaiah 34:4(Living Bible) The heavens above will melt away and disappear like a rolled-up scroll. The stars will fall from the sky like withered leaves from a grapevine or shriveled figs from a fig tree. Verse 8 - For it is the day of the Lord's revenge. 2 Peter 3:10 - But the day of the Lord will come as unexpectedly as a thief. Then the heavens will pass away with a terrible noise, and the very elements themselves will disappear in fire, and the earth and everything on it will be found to deserve judgment.

Since everything that is around us is going to be destroyed like this, what holy and godly lives you should live, looking forward to the day of God and hurrying it along. On that day he will set the heavens on fire and the elements will melt away in flames, but we are looking forward to the new heaven and new earth that he has promised - a world filled with God's righteousness.

Revelation 20:1(Living Bible) Then I saw an angel coming down from heaven with the key to the bottomless pit and a heavy chain in his hand. He seized the dragon - that old serpent who is the devil - and bound him in chains for a thousand years. The angel threw him into the bottomless pit which he then locked. Satan could not deceive the nations anymore until the thousand years were finished. God still has a plan for Satan, after the thousand years is over, that is so unbelievable. After the one thousand years, he must be released for a little while. We' will see this when we get to it.

Then I saw thrones, and the people sitting on them had been given the authority to judge. This is the church. I saw the souls of those who had been be headed for their testimony about Jesus, and for proclaiming the Word of God. They had not worshiped the Beast or his statue or accepted his mark on their forehead or their hand. These are the martyrs for Jesus during the tribulation. They all come to life again, and they reign with Christ for a thousand years.

When the thousand years comes to an end, Satan will be let out of his prison. He will go out to deceive the nations, called Gog and Magog, in every corner of the earth. He will gather them together for battle, with a mighty army as numberless as the sand along the seashore. Remember a few paragraphs back, I made mention of something unbelievable this is it. Satan will deceive many people, a number that cannot be counted. These people were born during this thousand-year reign of our Lord and Savior. The earth is the way God intended it to be before Satan deceived Adam and Eve. The people didn't know of Satan, but still this number is staggering when Satan is released. They know of the perfect world with Jesus in charge.

Then I saw them as they went upon the broad plain of the earth and surrounded God's people and the Beloved City (Jerusalem). But fire from heaven came down on the attacking armies and consumed them.

Verse 10 – Then the devil who had deceived them was thrown into the fiery lake of burning sulfur, joining the Beast and the false prophet. There they will be tormented day and night forever and ever. There's not much to say here other than what God's Word says from Verses 11-15.

The White Throne judgment is the second death, for those of you who never asked the Lord to forgive your sins and for what Jesus did for us on the cross. The Bible tells us that every knee will bow and every tongue will confess that Jesus is Lord. We can bow now in repentance, be forgiven, ask the Lord into our hearts, and let the Holy Spirit guide our lives through the truth of God's Word to Eternal Life.

John 14:1(Living Bible)Don't let your hearts be troubled. Trust in God and trust also in me. There is more than enough room in my Father's home if this were not so would I have told you that I am going to prepare a place for you when everything is ready. I will come and get you so that you will always be with me where I am. Verse 6: I am the Way the Truth and the Life. No one can come to the Father except through me.

2nd Corinthians 4:4 (Living Bible) Satan who is the god of this world has blinded the minds of those who don't believe. They are unable to see the glorious light of the Good News (God's Word). They don't understand this message about the glory of Christ, who is the exact likeness of God. There it is! We have to make the choice.

2 Peter 3:9 (Living Bible)The Lord isn't really being slow about his promises as some people's think. He is being patient for your sake. He doesn't want anyone to be destroyed but wants everyone to repent, Verse 10 - But the day of the Lord will come as unexpectedly as a thief. Then the heavens will pass away with terrible noise and the very elements themselves will disappear in fire, and the earth and everything on it will be found to deserve judgment. Just like a person who has been convicted and sentenced to die for the crime they have committed. They have to take that long walk to where they're going to die.

Let's take that long walk to the part of chapter 20 of Revelation 11 (Living Bible)And I saw a great white throne and the one sitting on it. The earth and sky fled from his presence but they found no place to hide. I saw the dead, both small and great, standing before God's throne. The books were open, including the Book of Life, and the dead were judged according to what they had done as recorded in the books. The sea gave up the dead and death, and the graves gave up their dead, and all were judged according to their deeds.

Then death and graves were thrown into the Lake of Fire. This Lake of Fire is the second death, And anyone whose name was not found recorded in the Book of Life was thrown into the Lake of Fire, forever and ever. Think about that – it's scary isn't it?

Chapter 21 – Here we are with two chapters to go. We left off at the White Throne Judgment. For those who don't know Christ as your Savior, and what Jesus did for us on the cross, and that this is God's provision for mankind - giving His Son for us - then you don't believe God's Word.

Psalms 14:1(Living Bible) Only fools say in their hearts that there is no God, if you're pushing all your chips to the center of the table, or if you're tossing the dice, thinking God's word isn't true. In Chapter 21:5 - The One sitting on the Throne said look I am making everything new! Then he said to me, write this down for what I tell you is trustworthy and true.

If you want to harden your hearts, you are buying a one-way ticket to Gehenna - outer darkness. The choice is yours. Verse 8 - but cowards, unbelievers, the corrupt, murderers, the immortals, those who practice witchcraft, idol worshippers and all liars, their fate is the fiery lake of burning sulfur. This is the second death.

The beginning of Chapter 1 - Then I saw a new Heaven and a new earth for the old heaven and the old Earth had disappeared, and the sea was also gone.

Colossians 1:15(Living Bible)Christ is the visible image of the invisible God, who existed before anything was created and is Supreme over all creation, for through Him God created everything in the Heavenly Realms. On Earth he made the things we can see and the things we can't see, such as thrones, kingdom rulers, and authorities in the unseen world. Everything was created through Him and for Him. He existed before anything else and holds all creation together.

Christ is also the head of the church, which is the body. He is the beginning, Supreme over all who rise from the dead. For God in all his fullness was pleased to live in Christ and through him. God reconciled everything to himself. He made peace with everything in heaven and on earth by means of Christ's Blood on the cross. We see and Verse 17 that he holds all Creation together.

So, at the beginning of Chapter 21, Jesus lets go of all the atoms, neutrons, protons, and electrons. Heaven and earth disappear. Then John saw the Holy City Jerusalem coming down from God out of heaven, like a bride beautifully dressed for her husband. God's home is coming among the people and God himself will be with them. He will wipe away every tear from their eyes and there will be no more death or sorrow or crying or pain. All these things are gone forever.

We aren't going to remember things, but we will recognize our loved ones. If someone didn't make it, we won't remember. The one sitting on the throne said, look I am making everything new! He also said, it is finished. I am the Alpha and the Omega, the beginning and the end. To all who are thirsty, I will give freely from the springs of the water of life. All who are victorious will inherit all these blessings, and I will be their God and they will be my children.

Then one of the seven angels who held the seven bowls containing the seven last plagues came and said "come with me"! I will show you the bride - the wife of the Lamb. So, he took me in the spirit to a great high mountain, and showed me the Holy City Jerusalem descending Out of Heaven from God. It shone with the Glory of God and sparkled like a precious stone, like jasper stone, clear as crystal (Jasper is a diamond).

Also, she had a great high wall with 12 gates and 12 angels at the gates, and written on them which are the names of the 12 tribes of the children of Israel: three gates on the East, three gates on the North, three gates on the South, and three gates on the West.

Now the wall of the city had 12 foundations and on them with the names of the 12 Apostles of the Lamb, and he who talked with me had a gold reed to measure the city, its gates, and its walls. The city is laid out as a square. Its length is as its breadth, and he measured the city with the read of 12000 furlongs. Its length, width and height are equal. Each dimension is approximately 1,500 miles square - about the size of the Moon, but not a sphere - making the base 2.25 million square miles.

Then he measured its walls, 144 cubits - about 216 feet thick. The construction of its walls was of Jasper (diamond), and the city pure gold like clear glass. The foundation of the walls of the city were adorned with all kinds of precious stones. The first foundation was Jasper (diamond) the second sapphire, the third chalcedony, the fourth emerald, the fifth onyx, sixth carnelian the seventh chrysolite, the eighth beryl, the ninth topaz, tenth chrysoprase eleventh jacinth, and the twelfth, amethyst.

The Twelve Gates were twelve pearls - each individual gate was one pearl, and the streets of the city were pure gold like transparent glass. Today, in 2020, the price of gold is 2,040 an ounce, and God made the streets of pure gold. It was nothing for God to do this. The ground floor alone would provide enough living space for more people than ever lived in the history of the world. But I saw no temple in it, for the Lord God Almighty and the Lamb are its Temple.

The city had no need of the sun or the moon, for the glory of God had illuminated it. The Lamb is its light. And the nations of those who are saved shall walk in its light, and the kings of the earth bring their glory and honor into its gates. The gates shall not be shut at all by day for there is no night, and they should bring the glory and the honor of the nations into it. There shall by no means enter it anything that the defiles or causes an abomination or a lie - only those who are written in the Lamb's Book of Life.

These last two chapters are kind of a mystery. God doesn't reveal too much about Eternal Life.

Chapter 22 is the last chapter. Psalms 34:8 (NKJ)Oh taste and see that the Lord is good. Blessed is the man who will trust in Him: Oh, fear the Lord you, His saints. There is no want for those who fear Him. Verse 10 - But those who seek the Lord shall not lack any good thing. Verse 15 - The eyes of the Lord are on the righteous. Isaiah 1:18 (NKJ) Come now and let us reason together, says the Lord. Though your sins are like scarlet they shall be as white as snow. Though they are red like Crimson they shall be white as snow. John says, for "Jesus at the well." Then there was the woman at the well, and Jesus said to her, if you only knew the gift God has for you and who you are speaking to, you would ask me and I would give you living water. Verse 13 - Jesus said, anyone who drinks this water will soon become thirsty again, but those who drink the water I give will never be thirsty again. I become a fresh bubbling spring within them, giving them eternal life.

Verse 29 - Come and see a man who told me everything I ever did! Could he possibly be the Messiah? Revelation 22:1 - and he showed me a pure River of Water of Life, clear as crystal, proceeding from the Throne of God and from the Lamb. In the middle of its street and on either side of the river was the Tree of Life, which bore 12 fruits, each tree yielding its fruit every month.

The leaves of the tree were for the healing of the nations, and there shall be no more curse, but the Throne of God and of the Lamb shall be in it and his servants shall serve Him. They she'll see his face and his name shall be on their foreheads. There shall be no night and they will need no lamp nor light of the Sun, for the Lord gives them light, and they shall reign forever and ever.

Then he said to me that these words are faithful and true. The Lord is saying that you can stake your life on His Word. The Lord God as a holy prophet sent his angel to show his servants the things which must shortly take place. Behold I am coming quickly! Blessed is he who keeps the words of the prophecy of this book.

When we see that it says it will happen quickly, the scoffer points this out. It's been over two thousand years. 2 Peter 3:8 - you must not forget this one thing dear friends, a day is like a thousand years to the Lord, and a thousand years is like a day. It's only been a couple days for the Lord.

What is being said is that when these things begin to happen, they're going to fall in succession, quickly and rapidly. God deals outside of time.

Verse 8 – Now, I, John, saw and heard. John said something similar in the first chapter. In 1 John when he said, we proclaim to you, the one who existed from the beginning, that we have heard and seen. We saw him with our own eyes and touched him with our own hands. He is the Word of Life. The One who is life itself was revealed to us and we have seen Him, and now we testify and proclaim to you that He is the one who is Eternal Life.

John once again fell down before the angel to worship, then he corrected John, telling him that he was a fellow servant. Keep the words of this book and worship God. He then said to me, do not seal the words of the prophecy of this book, for the time is at hand.

Then Jesus said, and behold I am coming quickly, and my reward is with me to give to everyone according to his work. I am the Alpha and the Omega the beginning and the end, the first and the last. He created eternity, past and present. He is the beginning of all things and he is there at the end of Eternity.

Blessed are those who do his commandments, that they may have the right to the Tree of Life, and may enter through the gates into the city. I, Jesus, have sent my angel to testify to you these things in the churches. I am the root. He is the beginning, the offspring of David the Messiah. He left his Heavenly Kingdom, took on the form of man to pay for our sins on the cross. He paid the price for us. We deserve death and the Spirit says come and let him who hears come, and who thirst come. Whosoever desires, let him take the water of life freely.

When Jesus started his ministry, He said come. John the Baptist was standing there with two of his disciples - one was Andrew, Peter's brother. John said to them behold look! There! There is the Lamb of God who takes away the sins of the world. When the disciples heard this, they followed Jesus. Jesus looked around and saw them following. "What do you want? he asked them." They replied Rabbi (which means teacher), where are you staying? Jesus said, come and see.

The next day Jesus found him and said, come, follow me. Then Philip went to find Nathaniel, and told him, we have the very person Moses and the prophets wrote about. His name is Jesus, the son of Joseph from Nazareth. Nazareth! exclaimed Nathaniel, can anything good come from Nazareth? What Philip's response to Nathaniel was then, holds true today "come and see for yourself."

As they approached, Jesus said now here is a genuine son of Israel. How do you know about me? Nathaniel asked, and Jesus replied "I could see you under the fig tree before Philip found you." Then Nathaniel exclaimed "Rabbi" you are the Son of God-the King of Israel! Jesus asked him, do you believe this just because I told you I had seen you under the fig tree?

You will see greater things than this. Then he said, I tell you the truth, you will see Heaven open and the angels of God going up and down on the Son of Man, the one who is the stairway between heaven and earth. That invitation is for us today. For those of us who are thirsty, come, "Taste and see the Lord. He is good." Let he who is guilty heed this warning from the Lord. For I testify to everyone who hears the prophecy of this book: If anyone adds to these things, God will add to him the plagues that are written in this book; and if anyone takes away from the words of this book, God shall take away his part from The Book of Life, from the holy city and from the things which are written in this book.

Revelation 3:20 - Behold I stand at the door and knock. If anyone hears my voice and opens the door, I will come into him and dine with him and he with me.

Dealing with this scripture is Luke 21:34 - Watch out! Don't let your hearts be dulled by carousing and drunkenness, and by the worries of this life. Don't let the day catch you unaware like a trap, for that day will come upon every person living on earth. Keep alert at all times, and pray that you might be strong enough to escape these coming horrors and stand before the Son of Man. Press on For the Cross of Christ.

Printed in the United States
by Baker & Taylor Publisher Services